SECRETS: A STORY OF ADDICTION, GRIEF & HEALING

~

TESTIMONIALS

"This compelling memoir takes an unflinching look at family, religious communities, and the self-destructive behaviors that can follow traumatic experience. Readers will be immediately immersed in the raw, moving story."

~ BookLife, September 2018

"I finished your amazing book! It absolutely blew me away! It is so fantastic on so many levels. I so appreciate having the opportunity to read it. What a beautiful book and so sad, but so well-written and full of wisdom. It is a gift; a gift to everyone. People who are helping people with addiction, people struggling with addiction, and people who have lost someone to addiction. It should be read by everyone."

~ Dr. L. Hermans

A must read! A mother's love brings an addict to life. Sarah is no longer another sad statistic. She is a loving human being caught in the throes of a terrible disease. Anyone dealing with any form of addiction should read this book. Most families have had to deal with this in some form. Alcohol, eating disorders, drug abuse, etc. I think there is dysfunction to some extent in most families, this book may help others to recognize the signs and symptoms to be aware of. It may also help others to heal and forgive, themselves and others.

~ Joy A.

"I read this book in less than three days and I had a hard job to put it down. I never cry when reading a book, but I did with this one. Beautifully written. I've passed it on to a family member who is also eager to read it!"

~Merlene F.

"I couldn't put her book down! She definitely grabbed my attention and kept my attention. I'm so sorry for her struggles but very inspired by her courage! As far as the grieving subject; she wrote perfectly! I felt her pain and could relate. Thank you for sharing Sarah's story. I think of her and how she opened my heart more towards addiction and how bad society has treated those going through the disease."

~ Alice C.

"This book touched home for me since I recently lost my son to an accidental drug overdose. It is beautifully written and highlighted the complexity of addiction. It shows how this epidemic can impact anyone. The negative stigma needs to be removed from this disease. Suffering families should not have that burden to deal with along with the grief. Thank you for this beautiful book. Hopefully it will help start the conversations and help end this epidemic!"

~ Kathy M.

SECRETS

A STORY OF ADDICTION, GRIEF & HEALING

ANN P. BENNETT-COOKSON

AUTHOR'S EXCERPT

"A dear friend, herself Native American, once told me that Native Americans believe rivers are sacred—the giver of life. My daughter's life is uncertain, hanging like frayed, loose thread. As her mother—I gave her life. Can I restore her brokenness, or at the least find those who can? Can I save her?"

~

https://mainelywriting.com

Library of Congress Control Number: 2018906948

ISBN# 978-1-73225-890-7

ISBN# 978-1-73225-891-4

 The story you are about to read is a memoir based on true events and presented from the author's perspective, although some names are fictionalized or omitted to express respect for their privacy and anonymity.

Dedication

This work is dedicated to my family, who are my world, and to someone who inspired me beyond words...

Say M. Rah.

CONTENTS

EPILOGUE

MARCH 2018

Nearly finished with this manuscript, I sat in a booth in a local café, reviewing these words, reworking, rewriting, revisiting, restructuring, adding clarification where I sensed ambiguity. I long for perfection, knowing there is no such thing. My first widespread published work, other than academic. Wanting this book to be the best it can be; knowing it is time to set it free. The trauma is revisited today because I rewrote the first few chapters. I've reopened the grief and am feeling Sarah's loss acutely. Remembering.

Almost three hours have passed. Somehow, I tuned out the surrounding sounds; people placing their orders, sounds of the machines as they ground coffee preparing cappuccinos and other caffeinated drinks, hot and cold. My own iced coffee is only half gone. I lost myself again; rewinding time in my mind; forgetting to plug in the laptop. Sirens just beyond the window, loud, insistent. Police and rescue trucks speed by. I cringe, instantly responding, unable to prevent the physical response to trauma. Goosebumps. I feel cold and shiver, despite the warmth in the coffee shop. It is four o'clock in the afternoon. I pack everything away, use the facilities and exit the restaurant to the parking lot.

Parked beside my car is a small silver sedan. In the driver's seat is a young woman who appears to be sleeping. Her seat is reclined. Her cell phone rests in her half-opened palm. Her face and lips are pale. Her light brown hair spreads out around her. Her window is half-way down.

Suddenly I am remembering a day in late September, a few months before Sarah died. Coming outside to take a walk, I came around the corner of the garage and noticed Sarah's silver Saab parked in front. She sat behind the steering column, her window open. Her eyes were closed, her seat slightly reclined, her mouth open. Her face and lips were pale. Icy fear washed over me. Walking over to the car, I reached in to touch her shoulder as I asked, "Sarah, are you okay?"

Startled from her stupor, she opened her eyes. She looked momentarily confused. "I'm fine. I'm fine." I knew she was not fine. I knew but I did not know what to do!

So, here I am again. Standing beside a car containing a young woman of about the same age as my daughter. I pause briefly beside her, then get in my car, slamming my door hard, hoping she will start and wake up, then start the engine—to just sit there. She is a stranger. What do I do? Rationalize that it's none of my business and she is probably just taking a nap? Ignore her? Drive away?

Glancing her way again, I notice she has not moved. Her eyes remain closed. Opening the car door, I climb out, approach her car, then hesitate. The decision is made. Remaining silent is not an option, but taking action is.

Inches away from her window I say, "Excuse me!" Silence. No response. Again, a bit louder this time, "Excuse me!" She startles. Her eyes open. Fear. I see fear. The same fear I saw in Sarah's eyes. Flashback.

Quickly, I offer reassurance. "I'm so sorry to startle you. I wanted to make sure you were okay. *Are* you okay?"

She attempts a weak smile. Responds. "I'm fine."

Somehow, I suspect she is not fine. Her eyes seem haunted, a bit vacant. What to do? I smile again to let her know that someone cares. She is not alone, yet she is. People are all around us. Driving in, walking into the café, then leaving. Paying no heed to a young woman who may have been just napping, but then again, she may have just used heroin. I know the signs now. I can no longer turn away. I want her to know that someone cares. I care. I am forever changed. Forever!

After supper I share what happened with my daughter, Heather. She hears the emotion in my voice, sees the glistening of unshed tears in my eyes. She rises from her chair to embrace me, holding me tightly as she says, "I'm so proud of you." Our tears intermingle as she whispers questionably, "I wonder if she was someone Sarah knew, perhaps got drugs from?"

"Oh, God, I hope not!"

Writing this story was not a whim, but a need. The purpose of sharing my story is simply this. To educate. To inform. To plead compassion. Understanding. To let other families know they are *not* alone.

The words in this story are mine as well as Sarah's. With writing, I've given Sarah her voice. Those with addiction and mental illness often feel alone and judged-stigmatized for their struggles. Judged as someone who has chosen to use illicit substances. However, is addiction a choice? Is mental illness a choice?

Will sharing my story allow others to more easily identify the symptoms of addiction and to recognize addiction as a disease? I hope so. That is why I am breaking the silence, using Sarah's voice, as well as my own with a clear objective: To de-stigmatize addiction.

Everyone's story is different. I can only share mine. The effects of addiction ripple out, washing over everyone in some manner or form. So, what should we do with the stigma attached to this disease? How do we lessen the stigmatization of addiction? How do we offer hope to those who feel hopeless? What you decide to do with this knowledge is your choice. Knowledge can be life-changing. One thing is a certainty. My life is altered and will never be the same.

Life experiences have allowed me to recognize something monumental, at least for me.

"We become what we think, so may we think positive thoughts, kind thoughts, peaceful thoughts, filling our world with light and peace. Our choices and thoughts are ours alone. We must be true to them."

JOURNAL EXCERPTS

~ SO MANY SECRETS WE HAVE KEPT. SO MANY TEARS WE HAVE WEPT. ~

Summer-2005

"Everyone has confirmed it for me; the fuck-ups will always continue. Those feelings—they are not real, insecurities. Take some drugs and get your life together, then you will be all set. For what though? What is next in this progression? My tummy tells me I need to eat. The mirror notifies me it is lying. I have eaten far too much, but I have not drunk too much. Where's that damn bottle?"

~Sarah~

2013

"Clearly, the banks have separate lobbyists in order to have all their needs met at the expense of their employees, customers and the general population of the United States today. Ridiculous! It feels as if I am swimming against the current and any moment the undertow will carry me away, but I keep silently strong against the hard, cold, salty waves slapping my face. I will not allow it. I have worked too hard, too long, going through too much to look back. Forward thinking is a necessary premise for ultimate future success. I would rather ride the train wreck and take the long way, A.K.A., the high road. This road gives you a high no drug will achieve. Drugs are like false promises; vacations from reality. Unhealthy, self-defeating behavior. Encouraged to destroy the impoverished so they can keep all their wealth and wield the power that accompanies it."

Love, Sarah

April 2016

"So, I made it to thirty. Woohoo! For a couple years, I didn't know if I would. What was the point? Struggling hard. I feel like I've forgotten all that made me happy—lost my reason to wake up in the morning—to have a voice—to care about anything…"

~Sarah~

WINGS

SHE SIMPLY FLEW AWAY!

A new curtain,
transparent and blue,
hangs in the window just for you.
A wind chime below tinkles sweet notes
with the slightest breeze.
I pause to listen-Yes!
I hear you!
Always near-
A whisper in my ear.
"I love you, mom-please don't cry."
Your voice fades away
with a sigh.
You took flight
on wings white as snow
despite my plea,
"Please don't go!"

~

PROLOGUE

Sarah died December 16, 2016 from an accidental overdose of heroin/fentanyl. Our family tragedy is not unique, but Sarah was unique. Our family is forever changed.

Sarah was so much more than someone struggling with addiction. She was a beautiful and intelligent woman who experienced a lifelong struggle with depression and anxiety. She struggled with self-acceptance. However, Sarah fought hard to live. She had hopes and goals for the future and worked hard to achieve them. Although she quit high school in her senior year, she obtained a GED, then jumped into college life. Her concentrations? Justice and Women's Studies. Focusing her energies on her studies was challenging for her, but she persisted—eight years of persistence. She attended her college graduation in 2013 standing tall, all smiles.

She championed those in society whom she felt were misrepresented. She longed to provide a voice for those who felt powerless to use their own. She loved horses and spent hours riding and caring for them throughout the years. Horses grounded her. She hoped one day to open a facility using therapy horses to help children with special needs.

She loved her family, her siblings, her nieces and nephews—

engaging with them often as she attended their birthdays and Christmases. Sarah wore many hats: a daughter, a sister, an aunt. Like everyone, she experienced successes as well as disappointments, joy as well as sorrow.

I was aware of her struggles; her conflicting emotions, but sadly I did not fully understand how heart-wrenchingly difficult Sarah's struggles were. She was deeply private and feared being misunderstood and therefore being misjudged.

Sarah had the kindest heart and a sensitive soul. Her lifelong search of love and acceptance consumed her. During the last few years of her life, signs of substance use disorder flanked her. I suspected, but I only saw a tip of the iceberg of what was really happening to her. She once told me, "Mom, you are in the dark, you just don't understand." She was right; there were so many things I did not understand. Her insight and intelligence astonished me.

Like many, I originally thought substance use was a choice, a deficit in one's moral code, a weakness that one should be able to control. Why must tragedy occur to inspire illumination? The reality is this; addiction is complex and those who struggle with it usually face other mental health challenges too. The scientific community identifies substance use disorder as a brain disease, something I did not understand or recognize until recently. Sarah was a textbook example. My knowledge comes too late for Sarah.

Writing this story has been incredibly difficult. As I began to write, my inner eye became focused, intent on rediscovering Sarah. The Sarah I knew as a child had long ago morphed into an adult I did not recognize or understand. I blamed myself. Where did I go wrong? In how many ways did we fail her as her parents? I wanted to understand. Will sharing my story allow others to understand addiction as a disease more fully? Will these words allow families to more easily identify the symptoms of addiction? In breaking the silence, shoving aside the curtains revealing the dysfunctionalI hope so. That is why I am breaking the silence, using Sarah's voice, as well as my own with a clear objective: To de-stigmatize addiction.

There is much talk on how to help those with substance use disorder. So far, though there have not been many success stories. People with addiction often neglect seeking treatment. Why? Because they are paralyzed by fear. Fear of facing judgement and punishment rather than help.

Perhaps it is time for redirection. Can we work towards removing the fear and the terrifying stigmatization attached to addiction and try something different? Let us direct positive energies toward these struggling souls. Rather than projecting fear and judgment, what would happen if society projected understanding, empathy, compassion and acceptance? Acceptance that they have an illness, not just addiction, but often, buried beneath the surface, acute sadness and unresolved conflict. Understanding the illness will then help us to offer more appropriate and timely treatment, rather than punishment within the punitive system.

As society begins to remove the stigma of addiction, boundaries to seeking recovery will lessen, improving the odds of recovery, decreasing the risk of death by overdose. My daughter's death must not be an ending—let it be a beginning—a beginning towards understanding, acceptance and empathy.

HAUNTING JOURNAL ENTRIES

"What joys today will bring. I would miss all those things I used to say I didn't like, because I really loved them, and if you could see inside my brain things would be so completely different. If only I could know what you really thought; what you've really wanted. I know what I want for myself, but I'm lacking the motivation to fulfill my dreams. Everything seems too hard and out of reach. I waste away each day closer to my last and without even realizing, I just waste them all away."

"I'm far from innocent anymore though. As hard as I try sometimes, I can never move back, only forward—onward in this march through time. And is it time spent, so-called wisely, that matters most in one's sinful lives or is it the silly moments—those moments we treasure our whole lives?"

"There's only one thing I've always wished for. To know the happiness everyone else seems to already know. To create a family that cherishes each other, instead of one that hates one another, and why? Why did we put up

with this; years of mistreatment, ill-spoken words spoken too frequently? Malicious attacks, for what? After all these years, it has taken us away from each other. Far, far apart."

~

"I feel closer to strangers than to the man who donated sperm to create me. Oh, a father is he—I beg to differ! A father should care for his children—wants what's best for them. He would never tear them down, especially not just to say he can. He stands up for them. Won't let anyone hurt them. He especially wouldn't do it himself. Above all though, he loves them more than he loves himself. A father, I have never truly known."

~Sarah~

~

FINDING SARAH

"I BROUGHT YOU INTO THE WORLD MY LOVE, AND I AM THE ONE WHO FOUND YOU AS YOU LEFT IT."

December 16, 2016

I found her mid-afternoon lying face down on the floor, her neck bent at an impossibly agonizing angle; the syringe still in her half-opened palm, her fingertips already turning blue. "Sarah, Sarah, Oh, God! Oh, God. Please, God, I cried out as I bent down toward her and tried in vain to turn her over. Although trained in CPR, I did not have the strength to reposition her. Tears streaming, gasping for breath, feeling anger and self-loathing for my inability to help her, I screamed downstairs to her father. "Call 911!"

The TV is on. He asks, "What?"

I am halfway down the stairs as I urgently demand, "Call 911!"

He looks at me stunned as I breathlessly say, "Sarah is on the floor, unconscious and I can't turn her over."

Turning off the TV he punches in those three lifesaving digits.

Moving as quickly as I can, I descend the stairs, rush past him, down the hall and into the office. I yank open the file cabinet grabbing the paper bag containing the Narcan, cursing myself that it is downstairs in the filing cabinet in the office, rather than where it should be; upstairs, nearby. Lifesaving moments lost! My inner thoughts in turmoil; "Stupid, you're so stupid, why did you leave it down there?"

Nevertheless, I know why it was down there. Sarah's sister Heather had it last and just as she was leaving to go home, she remembered it, pulled it out of her bag, and handed it to me. Reminding myself to bring it upstairs with me later, I placed it in the file cabinet in the office. I forgot all about it—until now, wasting precious minutes retrieving it. Wanting to race down the stairs like I once could but held back by something we all wish we could control—an aging body.

Roger seldom climbs the stairs, but he made his way up today. His joints, swollen, stiff, inflamed and painful he stood over Sarah, leaning on his cane trying to turn Sarah's inert form over from her prone position. The Narcan, a nasal spray, is in my hands. I tear it out of its package, but if we cannot get her face up, it is useless. His attempt to reposition her is fruitless while I sob in bitter frustration. Moments pass, just moments, before the front door reverberates with knocking.

I recall flinging open the door, allowing strangers into our home. First Responders. EMTs. Maine State Troopers, filling the narrow entryway with their bodies.

"Where is she?"

I sigh; releasing air, I have been holding in my lungs—not even aware that I have been restricting airflow. Sarah will be okay now. This is what these people do—they save people's lives—Sarah's life.

"Up there, in her room," I point, and move out of their way. They quickly climb the narrow stairway, carrying supplies, equipment that will resuscitate my daughter, restoring pinkness to her lips and fingertips. Please, please help her. Their presence is overwhelming. Fear washes over me, and guilt. So much guilt!

Her bedroom walls are still painted purple, her teenage choice of color. There is just enough space for her queen-sized bed, a nightstand, the mirrored dresser, her desk and an office chair, placed in the corner of the twelve-by-twelve-foot room. I bought the desk for her to use to finish her studies. She would study and journal for hours in this space. Today, she used this space to insert a needle filled with...poison.

There was no space for us as these men rushed into her bedroom —two Maine State troopers and two paramedics. We moved out of their way. Leaning on his cane Roger made his way to the bedroom across the hall—mine. I tried to join him, but my anguish and anxiety was too intense to sit down beside him, but for a moment. All I could do was pace, wring my hands, cry, and pray. God did not hear me that day. God had forsaken me.

Roger sat on the edge of the bed, unable to stand erect, his hands resting heavily on his cane, his head bowed. I watched anxiously as they tried to revive Sarah, hoping, barely able to breathe. Long, arduous moments passed. I observed Sarah's stockinged-feet moving with each chest compression. In an absent way, I noticed she wore mismatched socks. Her dark blonde hair spread around her now upturned face, filmy and messed. Her hazel eyes, framed with long dark lashes, now closed. Her face deathly white.

Listening as they tried to revive her, I heard…what? Laughter. They were laughing and joking as they treated Sarah. I glanced at Roger. "Did you hear them? They are laughing! They're cracking jokes!"

Roger looked at me with a shocked expression, then cocked his head toward the sounds coming from across the hall attempting to reassure me. "I'm sure they didn't mean anything by it."

I looked at my husband in disbelief. Anger. Anguish.

"How can they joke at a time like this? How can they be laughing?"

Tears streamed from my eyes. In this moment, I felt no comfort from this man who sat on my bed. My husband—married to for so many years. No comfort at all.

Was it less than an hour ago when Sarah came walking through the front door? Glancing at me as I stood in the kitchen, lifting her nose slightly to sniff the air, she said, "Hi, Mom! Whatever you're cooking sure smells good."

Turning towards her, smiling, I responded, "It's almost ready. We are having baked haddock, roasted sweet potatoes and zucchini. I'll make you a plate."

She turned briefly towards me, sent me a wan smile, but said nothing else as she climbed the stairs to her room. A short time later, I called her down for dinner, but she did not answer. Twenty minutes passed before I realized it, and I called her name again. I was not concerned at first. When she wears her headphones, she cannot hear me call her. Something began to worry at my mind, a sick feeling. I climbed the stairs to check on her, to find her not breathing, sprawled facedown across the floor.

Memories of that day are forever burned in my mind. Instant replay. Fear. Horror. Guilt. If only I had gone up to her room instantly when she did not answer me. My mind reeled with self-recrimination. Would things have turned out differently if I had urged her to stay downstairs and sit at the kitchen table as I served her dinner? If only...

It seemed like an eternity passed as minute after minute ticked by while they kneeled over Sarah performing CPR, administering dose after dose of Narcan, doing everything they were trained to do to restart her heart, to get her breathing again, to revive her pulse. I could not breathe. I sat beside Roger, then rose to pace—flinging silent prayers to a God I felt had been distant for some time now, but hoping, still hoping my prayers would be heard, granted. But in reality, who really has been distant, and from whom?

As endless moments passed, I finally heard words of encouragement.

"We have a pulse. It is weak, but it is there. We're transporting her."

I stood in the bathroom doorway. My breath left my chest as I gasped with relief. A trooper stood a few feet away, tall and muscular, much taller than my five-foot frame. He faced me explaining the plan.

"They are taking her to the hospital. But first, do we have your permission to search her room and her things?"

"Yes, do what you need to do," I tell him.

Another officer starts the search. Looking in her drawers, her closet, under the mattress, in a pink duffle bag lying on the floor. He looked through her worn, frayed wallet. No money. He found a credit card. An insurance card, no longer valid. Her driver's license. Her sister, Sherry had given the wallet to her as a birthday present a couple of years ago. She loved it.

"Hey, mom. Look, Sherry gave me a wallet. It is a Vera Bradley. Isn't it cute?"

I was going to give her a new wallet for Christmas. The trooper spied her cell phone on the desk.

"May I take this?"

I nod my head affirmatively, "Yes, take anything you need."

His eyes solemn he says, "We also need to ask you some questions. It won't take too long."

Chafing and anxious, I leaned against the door casing for support. The need to be with Sarah built, shoving away all thought, except motherly instinct to be at my daughter's side, but he blocked the stairway, my only exit.

Confusion assaulted me.

"Questions?"

Wanting to run, realizing I could not, I stood there meekly, obediently as I was indoctrinated to do. As a person of authority, he must be respected, and I need to be cooperative. Why didn't I just point to Roger, who sat silent on the bed, telling the trooper to talk to him because Sarah needed me? Precious minutes wasted as he asked his questions, which I did my best to answer.

He asked, "Do you know her dealer's name?"

My mind raced as I searched through the memories of revelations given to me in spurts over the past few months. Her sobs. Her grief. Her fear. Her despair. Revealing feelings of sadness so deep that my own heart squeezed with anger and despair. Something surges up, breaking through the surface of my mind. She whispers these words as she stands inches away. She hangs her head, then quickly raises her eyes wet with tears. "I was raped this summer mom."

Adrenaline, hot and venomous rushes over me. I am nonviolent, passive, but in that moment, I want to kill the man who hurt my daughter so. Instead, we walk into her room to sit on the edge of her bed as I hold her in my arms while she sobs great shuddering gasps of release.

"I couldn't tell you mom. It was my fault anyway. I went to the doctor for treatment. I handled it."

Inwardly questions rise. Why would she feel it necessary to handle such trauma alone? Why could she not trust me to stand by her, support her?

I recalled her words. "I remember waking up to find him on top of me. He told me that this is what I get for overdosing in his place. He saved me, and this was his payment. He was teaching me a lesson. He told me this is what happens when girls OD'd in his place."

This flashback receded as quickly as it washed over me. The trooper stood exactly where Sarah stood as she revealed her rape. Did she reveal that her rapist was her dealer? My mind has no memory of such affirmation.

"No, I don't know the name of her dealer," I told him.

How would I know that? Instead, stumbling over the words, filled with anger, I told him about the rape.

All the while, Sarah's voice rings in my mind, urging me out of the house.

"Mom, don't leave me alone with them. Mom I need you."

Sarah needs me. His radio crackled. He listened to a voice on the other end, and then held his finger up in the universal message as he said, "I will be right back."

He descended the stairs to go outside into the frosty winter afternoon, which had started out much warmer, the sky blue, the sun shining brilliantly. The light was already beginning to fade, edging from daylight to twilight.

This large man, a Maine State Trooper, his uniform official and dark, quickly climbed the stairs again to face me. I had not moved from my spot from the bathroom doorway, holding onto the casing for support. Roger had though. I had not noticed him pass by me, only inches away, to make his way back into Sarah's bedroom. He was watching the men searching her room, snatching up needles, wrappers, and their own paraphernalia used to bring my daughter back to life. They were putting things back into their cases. The officer opened a drawer, pawed through Sarah's gym bag. Opened her closet. Searching. Searching. Roger stood just out of the trooper's sight, still in Sarah's room, as he climbed the stairs to face me, his face a mask.

"Is anyone else with you?" He asked me.

I was confused. He knew my husband was here too. He had just spoken to him. *Why would he ask me that?* My eyes slid toward Sarah's room as I responded to his question.

"My husband is right there."

The trooper turned to face him, making eye contact, first with Roger, then with me. His voice was solemn. His eyes sad.

"I'm very sorry, but they lost her heartbeat. She is gone. They are taking her to the funeral home. Do you have a preference of where you want her taken?"

Confusion swept over me. Words rushed out.

"What? What do you mean? A funeral home?"

I could not understand why they were not transporting her to the hospital. I was unable to process his words and looked at him mutely.

Finally, my husband spoke.

"No, we don't have a funeral home in mind."

My inner thoughts raced. I was dazed. Shocked. Why would we have a funeral home in mind? Of course, we did not! She is not... dead...she needs to be taken to the emergency room, not a funeral home!

The trooper gently repeated that Sarah's heart had stopped, and they were unable to revive her. He repeated his words slowly, so our dazed minds could process that Sarah was gone.

No more smiles. No more shared confidences. No more birthdays. No more anything with Sarah. They apparently never left our driveway, but instead, struggled to stabilize her before they could transport her. At least, that is what we later learned. During those moments, as we stood there immobilized with shock, dazed with disbelief, our minds were barely able to process anything that had just happened.

The trooper named a funeral home just minutes away. "Is it okay if we take her there?"

Staring at this tall man whose gaze flickered from mine to Roger's, I am speechless, unable to respond at all. Roger was the parent who gave consent, consent for his daughter—my daughter—to be taken away, not to a hospital and emergency treatment. No, but to a place that smelled of death where strangers put her on a cold, metal table, covered her with a sheet, turned off the lights and closed the door where she lay alone.

Why is it that I did not think to ask to see her one last time? More importantly, could they not have asked if we wanted to see her before they transported her? Those questions simply did not come to mind in our shocked and numb state. My last memory of Sarah will always be of her lying prone on her bedroom floor, her fingertips blue, with a syringe still in her half-opened palm that fell to the floor as I tried in vain to turn her over to administer the Narcan. Would she still be with us if I had succeeded?

Somehow, I do not know how, my cellphone was in my hands calling my son and daughter, Donnie and Sherry, but neither answered. I was unsurprised realizing they were working. It was late afternoon. I texted them.

"Please come. Now. I need you. Sarah has overdosed. She is gone. Come. Now. Please."

My cell phone chimed. I answered. It was Sherry.

"Mom, what's going on? What has happened? What do you mean Sarah's gone?"

I became incoherent, sobbing uncontrollably.

"She's dead! She's dead!"

Her voice rises over the distant roaring in my head, in my ears, in my heart as I heard her voice rise.

"No! "I am coming. I am coming. I am on my way. I was in a meeting. I am sorry I did not answer. I am on my way. I am coming. I'll be there soon."

Moments later Donnie called. I had lost the ability to speak so handed the phone to Roger who speaks briefly to our son, explaining what happened to his sister. I heard Donnie's voice.

"Give the phone to mom. I want to speak to mom."

His voice cracks as he says, "Mom, I misunderstood. I am so sorry. I thought she had overdosed again. I did not understand. I am so sorry! I am on my way. I will be there as soon as I can. Hold on."

I was unable to talk. I was simply, overcome.

As I write, I am reliving the events as they unfolded that day all over again. My tears fall, fresh and new, but I am in control. I can do this. I must write. I must share. If I do not, I think I will step over the edge.

Falling. Falling. I cannot fall. I step away from the laptop. Tissues. A moment to regain my composure.

Your departure was sudden — no warning. I did not get to say goodbye or to hug you, telling you one last time how much I loved you before strangers lifted you off the floor to place you on a stretcher. They brought you down the stairs, out the front door, leaving our home for the last time. They loaded your still, inert form into the ambulance where your heart stopped beating forever, as mine rent in two. Shattered. Simply shattered.

That evening is just a blur. People came from the church to sit with us. Roger must have called them. They arrived before Sherry and Donnie. Two elders from the church with their wives, people I have known my entire adult life. Friends. Lisa, who was the first one to arrive with her husband, walked quickly, purposefully toward me and enveloped me in her arms. Holding me. Letting me sob. She stroked my hair humming soothing sounds; words are hard to come by at a time like this. What good are words? Just words. Meaningless really. What does one say when death comes? Too soon. Too young. Unexpected. A stolen, broken life.

Darkness had fallen outside. Someone had turned on the lights to stave off the dimness of a shortened winter day. The strangers are gone. We were now surrounded by people we know. Friends. Sarah's room is empty but for an unmade bed. Clothes strewn about, but no Sarah.

Sherry arrived. She wore a green parka. Her husband, Derek by her side. Solemn. Subdued. Our eyes locked, mine hollow and red. Sherry's were wide with shock. I was sitting on the couch beside her father. He was holding my hand, his arm around me, according to Sherry, who told me this days later as we rehashed that horrendous day. I remembered Sherry gathering me in her arms when she walked through the door. We held each other, rocking, crying. For how long? I do not know. We did not want to let go. I needed her strength, her warmth, the warmth of my remaining children, because now I have only three.

Donnie comes. Sherry steps away. His tall frame draws me close, encircles me, holding me tight. He is warm. His face is a rock. In control. His hazel eyes, so like Sarah's, glisten with unshed tears. My body shakes with sobs, harsh, ugly. His own tears fall; I feel their wetness as they drop upon my bowed head. He shudders as his own sobs come—once, twice, then somehow he pulls them back. Reining them in. Does he feel he must be strong for me?

My children are here. They will know what to do, because I am no longer present. My world has caved. Loss so deep, so cutting, it is beyond my sense of reason. A mantra erupts as I hear my voice, but it does not sound like me, as I appeal, "What am I going to do? What am I going to do? I do not know what to do! What do I do now?"

I hear my children's voices, but they are far away. I am in a river. The current is taking me away. I cannot think. I can only feel pain. In my chest. Deep. Cutting. Stabbing. Donnie and Sherry walk me to the other room, away from these people who are here to offer their support because Roger called them. Deeply religious. Uttering words meant to comfort. Resurrection. You will see her again in the new world. She is at peace. She is no longer hurting or suffering. It will be okay. Words I once uttered to others as they endured the loss of a loved one. I am thankful for their presence; at least I know I should be. I recognize they care, their concern, but emotionally dazed, they cannot give me the comfort that only my children can give. His family, his church family, surrounds Roger. His comfort. My daughter is dead.

The three of us—together. A moment. Family. Reconnection.

Finding solace in each other's arms. So many questions. The only one missing now is…Heather. Oh, my God! Heather. This will destroy her. Heather and Sarah, so close in age that once a stranger asked as I walked with them in a double stroller, "Are they twins?"

Two peas in a pod sharing so much and so many secrets. How will Heather react when she realizes her sister is dead? Will she come? Will she even speak to me?

Someone calls my sister, Brinna in California, and my brother, Rod in Bangor. Someone calls my oldest brother, Phil in Colorado. Who makes these calls? Roger? Donnie? Sherry? Brinna, who is a registered nurse, calls me later in the evening, but I am still incoherent. Shaken. Shattered. Stunned. I hand the phone to Sherry. I think I hear the word, sedative. No. I refuse. No drugs. No dulling my pain as Sarah did. I will feel…everything. I will file it away, keeping it. Cataloging it. For later. When the time comes. I will need these memories. No drugs to mask them making me forget. Clarity. I must have clarity.

However, in my dazed, shocked frame of mind, clarity is far away. Later, much later, with the help of others, I pieced together the fragments of that day. I do remember feeling these thoughts at that time. No leaving the house. No emergency room treatment by people who would not understand and probably did not care anyway. No drugs for me.

The evening grew late. Derek and Sherry are torn; wanting to stay longer, while realizing they need to leave, to go home to their own two children. Sherry focuses on her brother. Their eyes meet and an unvoiced message is conveyed. I hear Donnie's voice, but I'm drifting, disconnecting.

"I'll stay with them. I just need to go home for a moment to feed Rollo and get a few things."

Rollo is his dog, a boxer, high strung and full of energy. Crazy, bouncing Rollo.

Time has stopped in this house. Though my son left and returned, my memory is that of just knowing Donnie is here. Those moments are lost in my mind somewhere, settling deeply, irretrievable, a hazy, blankness.

He returns with his blanket. A pillow. He settles in the recliner. Silence is heavy, stifling, needing to be filled. He turns the TV on, volume low. Sound fills the dead air. His presence is comforting. What is he thinking? Will I die from grief and shock, the loss just too much to bear? Will I lose my sanity completely? Will I need hospitalization? I am numb. He stays, because tonight we cannot be alone. I am glad he is here, in our home, keeping us company. I feel so empty.

That night, lying beside my husband, not wanting to be alone, needing to feel his warmth beside me, our tears intermingled. Our loss heavy. Sleep was elusive, but it came eventually. A body can only endure so much, but it was intermittent, interspersed with swirls of color, then darkness as I drifted between sleep and wakefulness. Wakefulness brought realization. A waking nightmare that walks with me, that I must face, endure…somehow.

~

LEAVING

LEAVING FOR CALIFORNIA AND I DO NOT KNOW IF OR WHEN I WILL RETURN. SARAH, CAN YOU EVER FORGIVE ME?

February 14, 2017

The two-month anniversary of Sarah's death is in two days, two months since I found her in her bedroom. I have not heard her soft, musical voice for two months. In three days, a plane will land at the airport in Portland, taxi around the tarmac until it reaches the connecting ramp, unseal its door, and welcome the next flood of humanity to enter, to file down the narrow hall with wheeled luggage, backpacks, perhaps a toddler or infant. They will find their assigned seats, store their luggage in the overhead bin, sit down and reach for the seat belt. Click. Click. Click. The sounds of seat belts buckling reverberate around me. People with a host of destinations: New York, Pennsylvania, Florida, Michigan, Colorado, and California. The destinations will be as varied as the reasons for flying. Vacations, family reunions, business, illness, a funeral perhaps, or a death?

My ticket purchased. Destination: California, 3,000 miles away, as far away from Maine and Sarah's empty bedroom as possible. No looking back, no second-guessing. My intent is clear, focused.

Dear, Sarah: I leave behind your grieving father, who claims to have loved you, but for some unexplainable reason, could not easily express his love to you, rather just the opposite. His greeting was the same each day when you walked through the front door.

"How ya doing, Sarah?"

Your initial response: Silence. Your expression—a hint of disgust and disappointment. "Fine," you would mumble and head instantly up the stairs to your room.

If only he had looked deeper, would he have seen the longing and sadness in your hazel eyes? Would he have recognized the importance to reconnect, rebuild the fragile, shredded thread between the two of you?

It was not to be because he allowed himself to be engulfed and self-absorbed in his own pain rather than clearly seeing yours. It probably would not have mattered anyway by now. The damage was complete. The estrangement between the two of you had settled, firm, indisputable. A truce, but no connection. No mutual expressions of warmth or affection. Coolness. Distance. Acceptance.

His sorrow is evident, but is it sorrow due more to *my* coldness, anger and disgust directed towards him, rather than true grief for losing his daughter forever?

My grief consumes me. It singes me and fills me with indescribable pain and anger. My heart is shattered.

Sarah, I cannot be in this house, sleeping in a room just across the hallway from yours. I cannot be hoping you will come home soon, walk through the door, smile guiltily and say, "Sorry, I've been gone for so long. I just got caught up in things. I know I should have called you. Sorry, mom."

Sighing in relief, I pull you into my arms to hug you tightly, instantly forgiven.

"I'm so glad you're okay and you are home safe. Are you hungry?"

This vision dissolves. You will never come home again. I will never again hear your soft voice, even though I talk to you at night before I fall asleep, and sometimes, I think you hear me.

I carry on conversations with you in my mind, but your voice is fading.

"Let me go, mom."

We hug in my dream, tears streaming, as I ask you, "Must I let you go?"

"Yes, mom. You need to let me go."

Suddenly I am awake, hugging my pillow tightly, wet with tears. I still feel you in my arms and smell your sweet smell. The dream is so real, so present. My arms ache to hold you and tell you one last time, "I love you."

This house weighs heavily over me as the snow continues to fall softly and whitely, closing me in like a cocoon. Outside a blizzard is raging. The wind whipping up drifts of snow filling the cracks and crannies, piling up against the foundation snugly and tightly all around our modest cape home. The deck is a mound of snow pushing against the front door, cold and unrelenting. I was supposed to leave today but the airport is closed—all flights cancelled.

Boo-Boo, his sleek, black body draped across the back of the over-stuffed love seat, watches me as I type. Tears fall relentlessly, my eyes sunken and red. He jumps on the table beside the laptop and puts his paw on my arm. Scooping him up, he purrs loudly.

"He's a Tuxedo cat mom. He's very handsome."

The memory of Sarah's words uttered only a short while ago play back to me. His black and white coloring is reflective of a little suit with white fur on his chest, a black body and white paws.

Roger likes Boo-Boo now, surprising since it was not so long ago he was easily annoyed with him. Boo-Boo was aware of Roger's annoyance and would sometimes dig a claw into his arm or hand just deep enough to draw a tiny drop of blood. Once I told Sarah. Her response?

Grinning, she said; "Well, that's Boo-Boo's way of letting dad know he doesn't like to be treated meanly. When you treat him kindly, he will be kind too. Animals are much like people. Be nice and they'll usually be nice too."

Roger holds his stooped, ponderous frame erect with a black cane. His gait is slow moving and shuffling. He does not fool me. He can move when he needs to. His mindset seems to be that of a man rushing toward old age much too soon.

He will take good care of Boo-Boo. He cleans his litter box because my asthma acts up when I do. He made Boo-Boo a toy, attaching it with a long string to the ceiling fan. Boo-Boo bats it; breaking his boredom on these long, cold winter days. He talks to him in a soft, singsong voice and gives him fresh water and food. Boo-Boo is safe, warm and well fed.

Shortly before Sarah's death, I took to heart her concern for Boo-Boo as she implored, "Mom, please don't let Boo-Boo go out at night. One of these days he won't come back."

"All right, Sarah. I will keep him in," I reassured her.

I remember my promise, and I refuse to open the door despite Boo-Boo's annoying digging and crying at the door, insisting he go outside as the light fades into twilight, his favorite time to roam.

Boo-Boo is a magnet for trouble. I allowed him his freedom in early afternoon the day before Sarah's funeral. As mid-afternoon faded away, and the shortened winter day began to lose its light, I stood on the porch to call Boo-Boo back in.

The temperature was dropping, and the skies were overcast and gray. A snowstorm was on the way. No response; no black and white cat streaking across the road, into the yard to skip up the steps and into the door, his tail high. Intermittently, I opened the door to feel the cold air rush inside to call Boo-Boo, doing so until midnight, but he did not come home.

First thing in the morning, still in my robe and slippers, I opened the door. Snow was falling heavily, the deck covered with a layer of freshly fallen snow. A frigid blast of cold air swept inside. Shivering, I stepped onto the deck to call Boo-Boo again. Seeing movement beneath my car, I watched with concern as he crept slowly out from under the car. He painfully limped toward me, slowly climbed the steps onto the deck, then through the open door into the house. Somehow, he had made his way back home despite a deep gash on his hind leg, open, bleeding and full of grit.

I was afraid to lift him, of hurting him. He gingerly climbed onto the spare bed and laid down to lick and clean his wound. I took a picture of Boo-Boo's injury with my iPhone and sent it to Sarah's brother, texting him: "Boo-Boo's hurt. I think he needs to see the vet." Donnie came immediately.

When I called Dr. D., our elderly veterinarian, he asked if Sarah would be coming too. His silence was palpable as I began to cry. In-between the sobs, I told him, "Sarah died. Her memorial service is today."

Silence hung in the air, and a moment passed before his choked reply.

"I'm so sorry."

His voice held shock, surprise and uncertainty of what to say, but his kindness was evident when he told me, "I can see Boo-Boo in an hour."

Barely coherent, I whispered, "Thank you."

~Sarah, I know you cared deeply about Boo-Boo. I loved how you would gently hold him close to your heart as he purred happily. There was a symbiotic relationship between you two. You sensed when his need for affection was satiated, and you would gently lower him to the floor, letting him go. He would glance up at you, squeeze his eyes in a kitty way that expressed his love toward you too, and then scamper away. Boo will keep your dad company after I leave.

FAMILY HISTORY

Sarah is so young when she first starts journaling in 1999. Only thirteen-years-old, and she wanted to die. Her written words echo and crash in my mind as she described her intense feelings of sadness.

Words do sting and can affect our deepest psyche. How can a thirteen-year-old understand why her father is angry most of the time and why he lashes out toward those he professes he loves and should protect? How does she process all that negative energy that surrounded her, overwhelmed and confused her? Like mom like daughter—she began to write, but she wrote with intuitiveness and a purpose. Yay!

December 6, 1999

"Writing in a journal is purposeless unless you're trying to get feelings or emotions out. In my case feelings between me and my father that is so hurtful and complex they must seem simple to other people." *Sarah~*

February 2017, California

Tenderly I lifted one of her journals, a blue one, out of the suitcase touching its face. The surface smooth and cool. This small book, bound in soft imitation leather, its cover designed to present a sense of tranquility and peace rests in my hands. Blue water, blue skies and a single, white water lily floats serenely upon its surface. Kind of like our family, appearing peaceful on the surface, but beneath, dark undercurrents writhed, unknown and unseen by others. Secrets.

The cover on Sarah's journal states simply and clearly its purpose: Meditation Journal. On its inside cover is a quote by Helen Keller, someone who lived her entire life in the dark, yet her insight was astounding.

> *"When one door of happiness closes another one opens: but often we look so long at the closed door that we do not see the one which has been opened for us."*

FAMILY LIFE

Tears flowed in futility, shame and sadness as I began to read Sarah's words. Many doors have opened and closed in our family. To the world, we presented a beautiful cover, a perfect family. Week-by-week, year-by-year, cleanly, neatly, and modestly dressed, we would attend Christian meetings, presenting our finest selves.

The messages served from silver-tongued ministers varied in words, but the themes were consistent. One of which involved family life. God is orderly, and in his organization, everyone has a place. Christ is head of the congregation, but even Jesus is subservient to his heavenly father and creator, Jehovah. In the Christian congregation of this faith, men hold positions of oversight and take the lead. Women can proselytize in their communities, but the leaders in the congregation are male.

In the Jehovah's Witness family, the faith strongly instills the belief that the husband and father is head and lord over his family, his own private congregation. His wife and children, if they value their relationship with God, will submit themselves to this arrangement. The congregation, instructed by these dictates, feels that doing so encourages order, peace and happier families.

We did our best to comply with this arrangement, but home life was a contradiction to the appearance given in public. After attending Christian meetings at the kingdom hall (church), the smiles and dress-up clothing, now tossed away, revealed a family who lived each day in fear and anxiety. Tension often ruled our home.

I strived to keep the house clean and neat, not easy living in a small living space with four children. When the end of the day neared, we knew dad would soon be coming home from a long day at work—tired, stressed, and hungry. Anxiety increased as we wondered what his mood would be like. Would he come home smiling, or annoyed and angry?

REMEMBRANCES

The past rushes toward me... A family broken. Remembrances... I was too deep in the trenches to see... We were at war... Angry words and actions, flung about like knives, meant to cut and slash were omnipresent. God, what a mess we made of things. What was going on then?

Of course, there were happy times too. Our daily lives were not constantly in turmoil. There were moments when we laughed. There were family outings and events that were fun. However, as the children began to find their voices and articulate their discontent, tension grew. Those happier moments forgotten, washed away by a sea of discontent.

Up until the kids hit puberty, as parents, we seemed to be in control. Once in the dark, always in the dark. I seemed to wear blinders, outwardly accepting my role as a submissive wife, but inwardly seething with resentment and anger. I understand now what I did not understand then. I now recognize that I was exhibiting behavior identified by mental health professionals as passive-aggressiveness.

That was it! Control. Passive-aggressiveness. Puberty. We had hit a wall, including myself. We were sick and tired of all the restrictions put in place. Restrictions erected, done so with good intent, meant to be a source of protection, were now considered boundaries to be scaled. Good intentions simply do not cut it. By interpreting Bible teachings meant to be guidelines, we had set up roadblocks that prevented our kids from learning from their mistakes. Flexibility and balance did not exist. We thought by restricting them, we were protecting them. How wrong we were!

We had taught our children from infancy the dangers of "bad association." The church defines bad association as social contact with anyone who is not a Jehovah's Witness. In time, even within the congregation, members were careful with whom they chose to closely associate with. Why? Because of sermons given, describing there were those who presented themselves as Christian, but were wolves in sheep's clothing.

"Be on the watch for the false prophets who come to you in sheep's covering, but inside they are ravenous wolves." Matthew 7: 15.

Whom does one trust when paranoia surrounds you? What does a parent do when years later, secrets become known, as your adult children's latent memories resurface to reveal abuse by individuals within the church, people whom we, their parents, had trusted with something invaluable, precious and treasured—our children?

Our children were surrounded in a world of no's. No, you cannot go to dances. No, you cannot get involved in sports. No, you cannot have friends over, unless they are good Christians, (which we, as parents, were responsible to identify). No, to celebrating birthdays or any other holidays. Jehovah's Witnesses believe all holidays are pagan or political in origin and celebrating them damages their relationship with God. They use scripture to give credence to this belief.

As the children entered high school they were encouraged to further their education, but we were reticent due to our faith. The organization of Jehovah's Witnesses strongly discourage parents from enrolling their children in higher education. Jehovah's Witnesses believe that higher education can be spiritually dangerous. Why?

Because many who attend college leave *the truth. The truth* is a term that Jehovah's Witnesses use when referring to their religion. The church feels that associating with those who do not exhibit or encourage Christian conduct often result in a former Christian falling away from *the truth.*

I live with a lot of ifs. If, as parents, we had filled in those no's with more alternative and fun yes's, would things have turned out differently? If we had been less judgmental and more understanding. If only we had allowed our children to explore and test out the boundaries, offering our support as needed, rather than erecting walls they felt must be scaled. If instead we had built the walls with doors that led to opportunities to be explored rather than feared.

Hindsight as another truth comes to light. Higher education can be illuminating. Knowledge opens the mind to a host of opportunities and to a world seen in a completely different light. Education can remove fear of the unknown and broaden the mind to become more accepting and understanding, less rigid in one's thinking.

Opening the mind to alternative thinking can prove dangerous to a faith that narrows one's focus and thoughts however. It is difficult to find balance when one walks such a narrow and restricted line of thinking. A Bible scripture often used by the church to define this mindset.

"Go in through the narrow gate, because broad is the gate and spacious is the road leading off into destruction, and many are going in through it; whereas narrow is the gate and cramped the road leading off into life, and few are finding it." Matthew 7:13.

Many parents actively involved in this faith homeschool their children hoping by doing so they will better protect them from *the world. The world,* being society in general, essentially being anyone who is not a dedicated Jehovah's Witness.

Then again, many parents, regardless of religious affiliation, decide to homeschool their children in consideration of today's harsh climate, and often homeschooling can be a better alternative for some families. We however, chose to send our children to public school. We were confident that by indoctrinating them in this faith, they would make choices in compliance with the faith's teachings. Doing so indicated love for God and his teachings. Hindsight tells me that youth have more of an inherent need to please their parents rather than God. Thus, an ongoing inner conflict developed among family members. How does one rationalize behavior that seems irrational?

Church elders would often counsel, "Obey the faith's teachings, as well as your parents, even if you don't understand why. Be patient. As you mature spiritually, or as time passes, God will reveal more clearly the answers to your questioning thoughts. If you want to remain in *the truth*, you must obey its teachings." It takes time to achieve spiritual and emotional maturity. We simply ran out of time.

Meanwhile, I struggled with my own inner thoughts and questions. I believed that we, as humans, should use our mind to question and to expect rational responses, responses that seemed reasonable, that made sense. I did not understand why these thoughtful inner questions were not encouraged, welcomed. If we are created in God's image, would it not honor God if we carefully considered everything told us, not just blindly accepting it? There were simply too many no's. I do not remember many yes's.

As our children entered high school, their struggle to handle all these restrictions should have been glaringly apparent. Grades started slipping. Sullenness and resentment seethed. Was this just typical teenage angst? It seemed that almost every school day started with a battle. Mom was herding cats with an attitude.

"Get up. You're going to miss the bus."

A mumbled response.

"What do you mean you don't want to ride the bus?"

Refusing to ride the bus gradually evolved to refusing to get out of bed.

"Time to get up. What is wrong, I would query?"

The covers would be over her head. A muffled voice responded with one excuse or another.

"I'm sick. I have a stomachache. I have a headache. Can I please stay home?"

A new cycle began to emerge. School avoidance.

"What? Why don't you want to go to school?"

The cycle began to ramp up to other behaviors; pretending to go, but later learning the truth; skipping school. When they did attend school, other behaviors were brought to our attention. Heather seen smoking with a group of her friends on school grounds, and when confronted, her explanation?

"I was just holding the cigarette for a friend, so she wouldn't get caught."

Eventually, Heather and later Sarah, quit school altogether. Navigating this sea of newly erupting behaviors with peaks and troughs of emotions became overwhelming, for all of us.

FIRST IMPRESSIONS

When I first met Roger, I observed him to be a kind, supportive young man with a strong spiritual side. I was nineteen, recently converted as a Jehovah's Witness. He was twenty-one. There were glimpses of a troubled psyche that worried me at times, but being young, sheltered and naive; I dismissed these small glimpses of a distressed soul.

One day, I was hanging out with a girlfriend, also a Jehovah's Witness. The conversation turned towards my upcoming marriage. She asked me, "Are you sure you want to do this?

Surprised by her question, I paused for a moment to think about her question. "Yes, I'm sure. Why do you ask me?"

"I don't think it's a good idea. I don't think you should marry him."

"Why?"

"I just don't. You're still young, not even twenty yet. Maybe you should wait a little longer. Do you love him?"

"Of course. I wouldn't be marrying him if I didn't."

She looked into my eyes searchingly, let out a small sigh, then said, "Okay."

I sensed she wanted to say more, but held her tongue. She did not elaborate. I did not press her. I had made a commitment, a promise, given my word.

After our engagement was announced, there were moments when

disturbing behaviors would peek out, but then quickly retreat. These behaviors confused me. Jehovah's Witnesses are taught that we are all imperfect, which is true. Imperfection must be accepted, and we must not expect perfect behavior from each other. So, I forgave those momentary lapses when he would be unkind.

There were moments when I feared I was making a mistake, but Jehovah's Witnesses also teach that once a woman is betrothed, she has made a promise that must be kept. If a couple have agreed to marry, they have made this promise in the eyes of God. Breaking it would be wrong.

A TINY LEAF CAUGHT IN A MIGHTY TIDE

Early in our marriage, I realized our relationship was troubled, but Jehovah's Witness strongly discourage divorce. It is accepted only if a spouse is unfaithful. If I left the marriage, I could not remarry, at least not if I wanted to stay in good standing with the church. If I did so, I could face being disfellowshipped. Friends in the church could not talk to or acknowledge me. I would be ostracized. One day I swallowed my pride and fear. A hurtful incident with Roger occurred. I called my parents, crying and distraught with a request.

"Can I please come home?

The response?

"You've made your bed, now you lie in it."

As I reflect on those long-ago uttered words, if I had been pursued the conversation, opening my heart, poured out to my mother why I wanted to come home, would she have softened her response? Yes, I believe so. However, communicating to them the dysfunctional relationship I was experiencing was challenging. I did not fully understand it myself, let alone have the ability to articulate the relationship between my husband and myself. Emotionally, I was still an adolescent, naive and unworldly.

I just knew I was sometimes scared. I often felt humiliated and sad in my new marriage. To magnify the dysfunction, I felt shame and even guilt that somehow, I had failed and had done something wrong.

My mother's words stung. Stunned by her response, hurt and wounded, I hung up the phone.

Soon, I was pregnant. My choice was sweeping me onward; a tiny leaf caught in a mighty tide. There were eddies and there were whirlpools, but I was inexorably moving through life, as one pregnancy eventually led to three more over the course of ten years.

ANGER & REBELLION

Family life had now shifted, changed. Roger, who functioned best when he felt in control, was facing a new reality. Family members were rebelling against the No's and making their own Yes's.

Expressing his innermost feelings had always been challenging for Roger. He often struggled with expressing love toward his children or understanding why they questioned his authority. He never knew his father. Raised by an aging grandmother, one who struggled with her own insecurities and dysfunctions resulted in Roger adopting learned behavior: sarcasm and veiled insults bordering on hatefulness, impatience and frustration, which evolved into outbursts of anger. His anger seemed to erupt from the inanest situations, causing anxiety and fearfulness.

Our family life appeared to those within the congregation to be that of a strong Christian family with a father who was head of his household. In the Christian congregation of Jehovah's Witnesses, it is purported that Christ is head of the congregation and is a manifestation of love, treating members lovingly, kindly. What happens behind closed doors however, is not always evident while in public.

Time continued to pass, and now, at age thirteen, Sarah's three older siblings had gradually left the home. Sarah struggled with conflictual feelings of becoming a baptized Jehovah's Witness. Her reasons were evident. Our family life was complex and convoluted and the events that occurred with each child are stories in themselves.

Simply stated, one-by-one, each of Sarah's siblings ended up disciplined by the church elders. Why? Her siblings were baptized into the faith at young ages. Sherry and Donnie were fourteen when baptized.

Heather was baptized when she turned twelve. Youth is a time of growth, self-discovery, realizations, and with all of these things, yearning for something different, an emerging discontent.

Their teenage years were turbulent. One by one, Sarah's siblings were judged unworthy to be Jehovah's Witnesses when they developed relationships leading to premarital relations. Rather than resisting their body's fleshly longing for intimacy, which Jehovah's Witnesses are required to do if they are single, they allowed themselves to enjoy, *the pleasures of the flesh,* a term Jehovah's Witnesses often use when referring to sexual intercourse.

The faith considered them tainted and unfaithful to God. Their behavior was, according to church doctrine, disgusting in the eyes of God, and their spiritual relationship with God became seriously compromised. Now labeled as "bad association," the ultimate insult.

Jehovah's Witnesses base their doctrines on their interpretations of scripture. If a church member engages in fornication (premarital sexual relations), it can result in one being disfellowshipped, otherwise known as excommunication in the Catholic faith.

If a person in the congregation, including a parent, observes behavior meriting discipline, according to church doctrine, they must tell the congregation elders. It is a sin to keep secret any behavior observed or interpreted as needing the attention of the elders with the express intention to discipline the erring one. Not doing so endangers the entire congregation, tainting it.

Disfellowshipping keeps the congregation spiritually clean and is considered an act of love. They believe that disfellowshipping a dedicated and baptized member encourages the person to repent, turn around in their misguided, sinful path and come back to God.

To be disfellowshipped is the ultimate disgrace. A door shut firmly in one's face. Unless it involves a legal or emergency situation, family members cannot have anything to do with a family member who is disfellowshipped. Congregation members, referred to as the brothers and sisters, must not speak to the disfellowshipped person either. Some do ask for forgiveness and readjust their lives to meet the dictates of the faith, but many never return.

For those who are disfellowshipped, especially if they have been raised from infancy in a Jehovah's Witness family, such as ours, this is the only "family" they know and who they have relied upon for emotional and social support. Shunning by people in the congregation, otherwise referred to as *brothers and sisters,* as well as their family members, can be devastating. A disfellowshipped youth may feel forced to leave the home and left to fend for themselves without any support; financial, social or emotional. The results can lead to homelessness, loneliness, and desperation.

EPIPHANY

As I looked back in reflection of those turbulent years, I experienced an epiphany. Roger, always needing to feel in control, had lost control of his own family. I had approached the elders in the congregation and revealed Roger's abusive behavior causing his chastisement. His privileges as a ministerial servant (a step down from being an elder or leader in the congregation) removed. His own aspirations of one day becoming a church elder dissolved.

According to church dictates, if a man cannot control his own household, how can he accept the privilege of leadership over an entire congregation? I had spilled the beans, revealing dark secrets kept hidden for years.

GIRL TALK

A memory resurfaces as I write. When first married, I was asked a startling question by a friend, a newly converted *sister*. Jehovah's witnesses identify with each other as *brother or sister*. She lived close by—within walking distance. We were in my tiny kitchen drinking coffee, just the two of us. Our husbands were not present. Girl talk. A moment of shared confidences. Getting to know each other.

The walls were painted a cheerful yellow, as was the old farmer's drop leaf table that we sat at. The clock above the table, a wedding gift, ticked away. It was a kitty clock with a black and white clock face.

A long black tail was attached that swung with each tick. Its long-lashed eyes opened and closed as the tail swung.

Evidently, unnoticed by me, she had been closely observing how Roger and I interacted with each other. She reached out, taking my hands into her own as she asked, "Does Roger abuse you?"

Shocked, startled, confused and just a bit fearful, my denial burst forth.

"Of course not."

Her gaze penetrated deeply into mine. I knew she disbelieved me. Her question gave me cause for self-reflection.

Was our relationship an abusive one? When alone, I often cried and felt hopeless, helpless, especially after attending a Christian meeting. Was that why I often cried?

At meetings, I observed couples who seemed happy. My inner thoughts, difficult for me to articulate verbally, washed over me. I wanted to be happy. Why was happiness so elusive?

I simply had not reached the point in my thought processes to understand what she apparently clearly understood. Was belittling and demeaning speech toward me considered abusive? Roger felt the need to control finances. He questioned in depth all my spending. If I spent time with a friend or family members, he quizzed me extensively.

I did not, at that time, have the ability to process these behaviors as overly controlling or bordering on abusive. I simply accepted them because I rarely associated with anyone other than with families who shared our faith. I did not have a means of comparing my relationship or to even discuss it.

My mother had been in a similar relationship. These behaviors were familiar; behaviors I was used to. My new friend moved away shortly after. She and her husband's conversion as Jehovah's Witnesses apparently short-lived, as was our friendship.

FRUSTRATION

Roger began to focus his anger and frustration against Sarah and me, but primarily upon Sarah. Their personalities had never meshed, but this never became more apparent than now. She was thirteen. It is easier to express aggression and frustration toward a relatively defenseless young girl, particularly when her mom is at work. Secrets.

Donnie had previously been the primary target of his dad's anger, until one day, when he courageously ended it. At eighteen, taller than his father, and muscular, Donnie had reached early manhood. I stood, mesmerized, witnessing a cycle that was about to be broken, at least toward our son. There had been countless times when I had stepped between them to stop an argument. Not this time.

I do not recall what triggered Roger's anger. I do remember Donnie's response as he stood facing his dad who had raised his voice, and then his arm against him. The events unfolded so quickly, I barely had time to process what was happening.

Donnie maneuvered his father's position so that his dad's back was now pressed against the closed cellar door rather than his own. Donnie caught his dad's fist, stopping it in midair. Then he raised his own and let it fly, narrowly missing his father's face, instead punching a hole in the door behind him, leaving it cracked and broken.

Donnie's hazel eyes, hard as flint, stared his father's down as he ground out through clenched teeth, "Don't ever raise your hand against me again."

Donnie has since revealed that he has a recurrent dream of wanting to hit his father, but never allowing himself to do so. Why?

His words clearly articulated, "I do not want to be like dad."

Donnie is gone, newly married with a child of his own on the way. Sarah's oldest sister, Sherry is also married with a baby on the way. Heather, eighteen months older than Sarah, is living with a boyfriend, expecting their first child. It is only Sarah and me now in the home, alone with Roger. When Roger's anger and frustration blazes, Sarah is an easy outlet upon whom to vent his negativity and darkness. As he vented his anger and frustration towards us, ours grew.

HOPELESSNESS & FEAR

Shame washes over me as I remember those long-ago days when Roger's discontent oozed and seeped out, projecting towards us, but more often towards Sarah. Belittling, biting remarks. Intentions clear. To wound and hurt.

Our own frustrations magnified. He had also mastered the art of projection—throwing back at us his own negative behavior when confronted. Turning the tables; claiming we were at fault, that we were hurting him by expressing our feelings of anger and hurt. Our disillusionment grew leading to feelings of low self-worth and hopelessness.

As I began to share some of these things with others, many declared, "Why did you put up with it for so long? Why are you still with him?" I have asked myself the same questions repeatedly. It has taken me years to understand.

Attending college, sociology and human behavior classes, socializing with others, listening to their responses to my revelations, and hearing their own stories allowed me to better process and recognize the true nature of my life situation. Still—too little too late.

A woman who married young. A woman indoctrinated to believe that being submissive pleased God and maintained matrimonial harmony, as well as harmony within the congregation. A woman emotionally manipulated to the point that she did not believe she was intelligent enough to make appropriate life decisions, and if she attempted to do so, according to her husband, bad things would happen.

A woman whose spouse controlled the finances. The day came when he said we were going for a drive. Unaware of his intent, I went with him. The destination? The credit union. His agenda? To insist that I remove my name from his account. We sat in the car for some time as I incredulously asked him if he was serious. I felt rejected, cut off, demoralized, demeaned, bereft, and something else, anger! I asked him why?

"You're spending is destroying us."

My spending entailed groceries and necessities.

Later, I listened to him smilingly tell a friend, "it was the best decision I ever made."

He seemed oblivious to the demeaning and dismissive attitude he had expressed toward me. I was working two temporary part-time jobs. I quickly found a full-time job. But that meant, I was often not there when he got home from work.

When I finally had the means to purchase my own car, I was met with derision.

Believing I needed his support, I asked Roger to cosign on the car loan. He refused. I paid a visit to the credit union. The loan officer reviewed my finances, smiled and told me, "You do not need a co-signer. Your credit is fine."

When I told him they approved the loan, his words shredded, wounded me. His voice dripped with disbelief and venom. His derision scathed me.

"I can't believe they gave *you* a loan!"

He felt I had made a mistake buying the car; that it was a bad investment. I interpreted his response differently. As I reached out to achieve a measure of independence, of self-worth, did he somehow feel threatened?

A purple Grand Am with a spoiler. Such a beautiful car. When I drove it to work each day my heart lifted. For me, a car meant freedom. As I zoomed down the highway, I felt as if I were flying. I was in the driver's seat. I was in control. What a wonderful feeling! Roger's control over me was crumbling.

I worked hard and paid the loan off early. Still, all those years of being under a man's complete control and emotional manipulation had taken an immense toll. Our family had paid a terrible price. I had had enough.

Approaching the church elders again, I tearfully poured out my heart, swallowing my shame. The belief that revealing these secrets was somehow expressing disloyalty toward my husband lingered but remaining silent was no longer an option for me. Sarah and I needed their help. I hoped they would reason with Roger, redirecting him with spiritual counsel, a belief system Roger expounded to others in his own proselytizing, yet could not successfully practice toward his wife and children. Love, respect, kindness, compassion.

Their advice: God's word instructs that a wife must be submissive and honor her husband as her lord. The wife must be respectful.

Told, "If you listen to him and do what he says everything will be fine."

Yes, he received counsel that if he wanted my respect he must treat me kindly, as well as the children. My emptiness grew, my faith continued to weaken. Hopelessness settled in.

The only child left in this house now was Sarah. Patterns of behavior had set in and changing them was an uphill battle and seemed impossible. The damage and the results: devastating.

I did the unthinkable. I went outside of the church, seeking help from the community. I called a domestic abuse hotline, arranging to meet with a local agency for advice. Referred to a counselor; she listened, provided validation and guidance. I was given encouragement and strength, things I did not receive from men of oversight in my own religion. Things I desperately needed.

I finally mustered the courage to have Roger removed from the house. Sarah watched as her dad opened the door to a state trooper who held court papers. "

Your wife seems to mean business. She has filed a grievance of abuse and here are the details. You need to leave the premises immediately. Are there any firearms in the house?"

Sarah is sixteen. She flashed a triumphant grin at her dad's back as the officer escorted him out of the house, an armed presence, the only way I could get him to leave. I was hiding, with Sarah's knowledge, in a hotel. I had been there for two nights. Sarah could have come with me, but she refused.

"Mom, I want to be there when they make him leave."

Would things have turned out differently for Sarah if I had stuck to my guns and kept my backbone, not allowing myself to succumb to fear?

MISGIVINGS

Two months passed, Sarah had a boyfriend. He was hanging out at the house a lot. He was nice enough, but his presence was unsettling. I was experiencing misgivings. Missing the comforting feeling of a male presence but forgetting how overbearing his presence had been. Married for more than twenty-five years, I had always had a partner. The house felt different now. Whether I was ready to admit it or not, I felt lost, empty. Bereft, unsafe.

Winter was approaching. The car needed maintenance. The oil tanks needed filling. I needed the snow tires installed. Roger had always taken care of these things. Could I afford to pay someone? How was I going to pay the bills? Self-doubt reared its ugly head—again. I caved.

I decided to meet with Roger to explain how his long-lasting abusive behavior had forced me to have him removed from the home. He reassured me that he loved us, and he was sorry he had been hurtful. He seemed to be genuinely contrite. He seemed to take ownership of his behavior and willing to accept the need to change it.

Counseling was court mandated. He agreed to the terms. With trepidation, I reversed the order in front of a judge, with Sarah sitting beside me, tears streaming down her face.

What...had...I... done?

Did I just seal your fate, or was destiny simply enveloping you, something I could never know? Because, again, much later, I came to realize this boyfriend was one of your firsts...first sexual experience...first exploration into drug use. Too little, too late.

~

BUT, I DID FIND YOU

MAYBE THAT IS WHAT YOU WANTED. YOUR DOOR WAS HALF-OPEN, NOT CLOSED AS IT USUALLY WAS...

Sarah, did you hope I would find you, like before? How were you to know that this time would be different? Informed it was a "bad batch," mostly fentanyl — enough to kill ten times over! As you injected the needle and pushed the syringe down, the lethal mixture rushed into your veins, reaching your heart in seconds. You dropped from your chair, landing face forward on the floor. You were sitting so closely to the wall that there was not enough room for your tall frame. Your neck bent at an angle as your head rested against the wall. I choose to believe you lost consciousness instantly. You felt no pain, did you? I did not hear you as your body hit the floor, upstairs in your room, alone, the syringe still in your half-opened palm, while we were eating dinner, unaware you were dying.

A TRIAL RUN

Was it only a few weeks ago when I heard unusual sounds from Sarah's room? Heavy labored breathing, loud and gasping through her closed bedroom door. I pushed the door open to see Sarah slumped in her desk chair.

Oh, God, no! Her lips were tinged whitish blue.

"Sarah, Sarah, can you hear me?"

I shook her, and she moaned. Her eyes fluttered, opening briefly, confused, and disoriented, then closed again. I rushed downstairs, running past Tierra, who was sitting on the air mattress in the living room. Our grandchildren were visiting. Tierra, thirteen and her brother Garry, fifteen. I hurried down the hallway and burst into Roger's bedroom. Garry was at his computer in the office at the end of the hall. Roger was sitting on his bed strumming his guitar. Terrified, words burst from me, "I think Sarah is overdosing."

Roger looked at me in shock asking, "What do you mean?"

Briefly, I gave him the details, and then rushed back to Sarah's side. Tierra had already run upstairs to her aunt's side. She was shaking Sarah. Sarah was confused, but awake. Part of me was filled with consternation that Tierra was present and observing, amid this drama, a terrifying event that a thirteen-year-old should never experience. I did not want her there, seeing her aunt in such a state. I am powerless. It all unfolds so fast.

Flinging a silent prayer, not fully realizing this event was a prelude signaling Sarah's eminent death in just two short weeks, I was only grateful that I was there to revive her before it was too late.

The following two hours were agonizing as I tried to reason with Sarah, begging that she let me take her to the hospital. Her response?

"Mom, I'm sick. I not getting in the car."

Then she rushed into the bathroom to vomit repeatedly vile, black, disgusting nastiness.

While she purged death, I grabbed the syringe and the spoon, still containing residue of the drug. I quickly searched her room for other drugs and found bags of pills and syringes and confiscated them, hiding them as she continued to purge the drugs from her system.

Later, I had the baggies full of pills analyzed.

"Forms of marijuana," they explained. "Not heroin."

I never gave them the spoon I found, still containing a bit of residue. I hid it and neglected to bring it with me when we met with these strangers, people I prayed would offer answers, guidance and the hope of finding Sarah treatment and recovery.

Why, Sarah? Why? A parent's nightmare is now my reality. Guilt and despair overwhelmed me. *I failed you.*

Minutes. An hour. Then two hours passed as I tried in vain to reason with Sarah, but she was adamant in her refusal to seek medical attention. As she continued to vomit, I called the Crisis hotline, terrified, barely coherent. A woman answered. Among her multitude of questions, she asked; "Are there any children in the home?"

Fearful of what may happen to my two grandchildren who are staying with us while I settle them into homeschooling I hesitate briefly, then... I lie. "No."

I am not thinking rationally. I do not clearly understand at that moment why she asked me that question. My instincts are only to protect, but our world is spinning out of control.

She urged me to get Sarah to the emergency room, explaining that though she is somewhat coherent, she could still be in danger. She asked to speak to Sarah.

Eventually, when I gauged that she could understand, I explained to Sarah that crisis workers wanted to talk to her. Sarah shook her head no-no! She was still bewildered and confused.

I told her, "YES! You must speak to them or they will send police and paramedics."

Her eyes widened in fear. Reluctantly, she took the phone. Even these people, supposedly trained in the art of negotiation, could not get through to her. She refused treatment, forcing them to call authorities.

Police and EMTs were knocking at the door within moments. Roger opened the front door allowing them to enter into the living room. It was one a.m. Two EMTs and three uniformed officers, two male and one female entered. Too many bodies in too small a space. Intimidating. Overwhelming. Suffocating. Guns in holsters strapped to their waist.

Their eyes circled the room, taking in the scene before they focused on Sarah. She stood fearfully a few feet away, leaning against the kitchen table, her arms folded across her chest. Her face was pale, and her dark blonde hair hung limply. Her eyes were dark pools, reflecting fear and suffering. Her ability to find the strength to stand there after what she had experienced astounded me. Her resistance angered and deflated me.

Articulately defiant, she stood steadfast in her refusal of treatment.

Her words?

"I'm okay. This is a family matter. I am fine. I'm still breathing."

Tierra sat in the recliner facing the front door where these strangers stood, silently watching, listening. I stood behind Tierra, just a few feet from Sarah. Sarah's dad sat on the couch centered in front of the living room windows. His legs spread apart, shoulders slumped, his head hanging low. Garry stayed out of sight in the office at the end of the hall, where a twin-sized bed had been set up, silent, but listening. He was in front of his computer, edgy, fearful, and uncertain of what to do. He messaged his stepbrother.

"Tell mom, Sarah is in trouble. She overdosed. Cops and EMTs are here."

One EMT, youthful in appearance, but eyes that reflected otherwise; someone who has seen things that most of us will not see in a lifetime. He addressed Sarah.

"I can see you've taken something. Your eyes show that. Let us check you out. We're here to help you."

Her posture was defensive as she silently shook her head.

One of the police officers tried to reassure Sarah.

"You're not in trouble. We are here because we want to make sure you are okay. You are not our first call tonight. There have been several others before you. People have died tonight. There is some bad stuff out there and you might have gotten some."

Sarah looked at them with mistrust. This was not her first rodeo. She knows the drill. She has seen her friends arrested and charged with possession. The governor of Maine is more interested in punishment than treatment and this outlook carries through into the mindset of law enforcement and society in general. She is aware that

Maine has limited resources to help people like her, people who are deep in the throes of opioid addiction. Unlike me, who at that moment I still believed in the system. I naively thought that one only needed to ask for help and it was easily given.

Hundreds of people are dying in Maine, from what is now recognized and labeled as an opioid crisis. Each year the number of deaths increase as the formula changes because stronger, more powerful drugs are used that not only provide a more intense euphoria to the user, but also causes heroin to become more lethal.

Those responsible for the distribution of heroin have introduced other synthetic components into the mixtures such as fentanyl and Carfentanil. This is a synthetic narcotic analgesic produced from morphine, but it is 10,000 times more potent than morphine and 100 times more potent than fentanyl, which itself is 50 times more potent than heroin. Carfentanil was never intended for human use due to its toxicity.

In 2016, there were 376 deaths directly connected to opioid overdoses in Maine; Sarah was one of them, number 374. Sarah became a statistic, a number. To us, she is more than that, so very much more. Timely and appropriate treatment for addiction in Maine, especially as it is mostly a rural state, is challenging and extremely limited, especially for those without insurance. Adding to this tragedy, the governor of Maine chooses to focus more on punitive action rather than treatment, while families like us watch loved ones die.

"It's an epidemic," the media says. Newspapers publish articles. Local newscasts feature the growing opioid problem in Maine. Grieving faces flash briefly across the screen. I never dreamed that soon I would become one of them.

Where are the answers to the problem? What are the solutions? Grieving families silently walk among us. We avert our eyes. Who wants to gaze into, let alone acknowledge eyes reflecting sorrow and hopelessness? We pretend that this problem will go away if we do not acknowledge it. Or, we are simply too traumatized, too stricken with the pain of losing someone we love.

The pain of speaking about it is overwhelming, all-consuming. We freeze our hearts, numb our shocked minds, distract ourselves with the infinite number of things involved in daily living.

Then, there are *the others*; those who take to their beds in grief unable to function. I am determined to not become *the others*. Determined to not freeze my mind. Determined to use my voice, my words and open my heart to—a painful new reality, and somehow strive to make a difference in some small way.

Some voice their hate and disgust.

"These addicts deserve what they get. Let them die! They are a burden to society and even their own families."

My own ears have heard such comments; my eyes have read them. I do not bow my head in shame. I refuse to hate.

So much bias, but so little knowledge, compassion or understanding. I wonder, would these individuals voicing hate and disgust toward those with opioid dependence change their opinion if they were looking through the eyes of a family member, standing in my shoes experiencing a living nightmare?

Anguished, my voice shaking, I asked the EMT a question.

"What help *is* out there?"

He shook his head negatively.

"Not much."

My heart plummeted. Though I struggled to regulate my breathing, I refused to break eye contact. He paused appearing to give my question further thought.

He remembered someone connected to law enforcement in a nearby coastal town who was developing a program to treat addiction. He gave me his name and phone number. Catching my breath, I snatched at this crumb, this tidbit of hope, writing the information on a scrap of paper, stuffing it in my pocket.

Was that concern I saw reflected in their eyes as they continued their attempt to reason with her? I remember someone uttered these words that night, but I do not remember which person voiced them. Was it one of the officers or one of the EMTs? It does not matter, but the words stuck.

"You are still alive…this time. We are thankful for that, but the cat is out of the bag now. Your addiction is no longer a secret. This is not the first time we have been here at this address when you called for help for your boyfriend. Yes, it is a family matter, but it is also a life and death matter. If you don't seek treatment soon…"

His sentence trailed away, unfinished, unvoiced.

My gaze swiveled back toward Sarah as I struggled to take in his words, processing them. Her face crumbled, but she stayed mute, unrelenting in her continued refusal of treatment. *Why, Sarah? Why?* Questions. So many questions.

All of us were defeated that night. Sarah, her family, the police and the EMTs. Lines of defeat and exhaustion etched our faces. I watched them silently file out of our home. Dread, hopelessness and fear descended. A pall lingered. Dark. Foreboding.

Someone locked the front door and turned off the outside light. Sarah headed upstairs, her little entourage following behind her, Tierra and me. She laid down on her bed, Tierra beside her. I sat on the bed close to Sarah, holding her hand tightly.

This thirteen-year-old woman child held Sarah in her arms, her own tears falling, as Sarah sobbed, repeatedly apologizing to her.

"I'm so sorry. I am so sorry. You never should have seen this. You were not supposed to see this. I'm sorry."

Sarah spoke this mantra repeatedly as she sobbed in despair, "I'm just so sad. I'm so, so sad."

Our faces were wet with tears. Gradually Sarah's sobs subsided as exhaustion overcame her and she escaped briefly from her pain, falling asleep, her breathing becoming deep and regular.

It is 2:30 a.m. Making my way to the bathroom, shaking, crying, I scrub away all the vileness that spewed from Sarah's body. Although she tried to clean it herself, in-between her vomiting, much of it remained. On the walls, the toilet, the floor. Tierra was on my bed sobbing as she talked on the phone with her mom, Sarah's sister, Heather. At 3:30 a.m., the house was finally silent. Emotionally exhausted I eased into sleep; my dreams ominous, dark and writhing.

Roger and I took Garry and Tierra home the next day. Home-schooling was over in our home. Priorities were set. Responsibilities shifted as we focused completely, unequivocally on Sarah. The clock was ticking. Time was growing short; we just did not know how short the time was for Sarah. A trial run…

TOO LITTLE, TOO LATE

After finding Sarah in her room the first time just before Thanksgiving on the brink of overdosing, fear set in—dark, forbidding, overwhelming. It swept over me like an unstoppable wave.

Roger and I began frantically searching for treatment options for Sarah. We spent several days online and, on the telephone, only to be challenged by roadblocks. Call after phone call we were always asked the same question.

"What insurance does she have? Oh, I'm sorry; we don't provide treatment for the uninsured."

The one phone call that filled me with the most disgust resulted from information I found online, falsely indicating a link that would provide addiction treatment information, specifically for Maine residents. Instead, it connected us to a salesperson representing a California residential addiction treatment facility. Setting the phone to speaker, Roger sat and listened, as I engaged the person in conversation.

The man was smooth, knowledgeable and relentless. He informed me of the dangers of drug addiction (As if I did not already know!) He expounded how this program would help our daughter. His final hook?

"You know if you don't do this she might die."

The cost of their program was $35,000 plus plane fare to and from their facility.

Shocked, I told him, "We don't have that kind of money."

After listening to him for several more minutes, he informed us they could provide direct financing if we agreed to put up our home as collateral to pay for treatment.

"It's a sales pitch," Roger said.

He got up from the table and walked away. I pushed the end button, lowering my head into my arms, feeling defeated.

A few days after Sarah's memorial service the salesman called to follow-up on our conversation, asking if we had given the conversation more thought and what we had decided. He asked, "Are you ready to move forward?"

"Sarah died a week ago," I sobbed into the phone.

A moment of shocked silence passed before he uttered, "I'm so sorry."

Three simple words that were meaningless, empty. I ended the call as grief washed over me, and anger. I wonder about this man as I write. Did he later reflect on our conversation? Did Sarah's death have any effect on him at all?

Determined to find Sarah some sort of treatment, we called the local hospital. They had an in-house treatment program, but the waiting list for treatment was months long. They could fit Sarah in for a screening, but not until January. Not realizing this appointment would never materialize, I set up the appointment.

I asked them for any other referrals. Anything? We were given a name, Wellspring, located in Bangor, which was an in-house long-term treatment facility. We called them immediately and asked them to fax an application. We researched Wellspring in more depth and printed out information, attached the application and left it on the kitchen table for Sarah to see. However, it takes time for the bureaucratic wheels to turn. More importantly, Sarah needed to be cooperative and accept treatment.

That night I awoke in the wee hours of the morning to the sound of murmuring voices downstairs, then the sound of sobbing. Was that Sarah crying? Heather's voice floated upstairs, soft, comforting. She was with her sister. Exhausted. Knowing she was not alone, I succumbed to fatigue.

When I awoke in the morning, Sarah was gone. Entering the kitchen, my eyes went directly to the spot where I had left the papers. They were no longer on the table but were now on the buffet. The application was on top of the packet, face down. Heather later told me that Sarah had read it and had become anxious, agitated. She voiced her fears to her sister; fear that we did not love her, fear that we wanted to send her away.

Finally, remembering the contact number the paramedic had given us, we called it, only to get a voicemail, so we left a message. Later that evening the phone rang. The man on the line was the Chief of Police who worked for a neighboring town. As we spoke with him we recognized his sincerity, his kindness, his insight. Though a police officer, he was also one who recognized those with addiction needed treatment, not judgment and fear of arrest. He began to restore my hope. He briefly outlined the program to us. What drew me was his assurance that the program was not connected to law enforcement, despite his attachment to it. Those reaching out for help did not need to fear punitive action. No fear of arrest or incarceration. He invited us to meet with him. He explained we would initially speak with a volunteer, a woman who was personally touched by addiction, whom he referred to as one of his *angels*. He gave me her phone number. I called her that evening, setting up the meeting.

The biggest challenge now; how to get Sarah on board?

I approached Sarah the next day.

"Sarah, we've found a program close by and it is free, so no worries about how to afford paying for this."

Sarah looked at me with accusation.

"You mean you just did this without talking to me first?"

In an effort to reason with her I reminded her of a conversation we recently had.

"Do you remember when we talked about finding treatment the other day? You said there was not anything affordable, especially since you have no insurance. Remember how I told you, I didn't know what was out there, but I was going to find out?"

Sarah nodded.

"This is what I found out. I called the number the EMT had given me the other night. I learned there is a program to help treat those with opioid addiction quite near us. The Chief of Police sponsors the program, and although we will be meeting someone in the lower level of the jail, the individuals we will be speaking to are not police. I was assured this program is a separate entity from enforcement. There is no cost, no judgments. They offer treatment options until you can find long-term treatment."

Ever distrustful, especially with anyone who appeared to be connected to the penal system, she refused to go.

Desperate and frightened for Sarah, Roger and I decided to go without her. We awoke that morning to a beautiful day, brilliantly sunny, the sky deep blue that stretched toward eternity. I wished I could lose myself in all that blueness. It was late November. The temperature in the low fifty's, rare for Maine. Was this an omen of hope? When we arrived, a petite, middle-aged woman greeted us. She smiled warmly. She took my hand squeezing it gently as she said, "I'm so glad you came."

She began the conversation by sharing some of her own story of a daughter also caught in the sticky web of addiction. We slowly, hesitantly, painfully shared our own. She explained there was someone she wanted us to meet. He was highly respected in the community as a professional drug abuse counselor who worked with them in the program. We agreed.

A tall, older man with thinning grey hair entered the office. Introductions were made. He expounded his credentials, his experience, his own familial experience with addiction.

The interview went quickly as he asked us several questions to get a feel of our family history and of Sarah.

Looking at us directly he asked us, "Why is it your daughter would not come?"

His eyes slid from Roger's face to my own. A pause in the conversation ensued. I waited for Roger to respond, but he remained silent. Clearing my throat slightly, I attempted to explain.

"When I explained to Sarah the Chief of Police sponsors the program and that we'd be meeting at the police station she became suspicious, anxious and fearful. She distrusts the police. She has had negative interactions with police in the past. Then, when she realized her dad would be present too, she outright refused because she won't ride in the car if her father is present."

His attention focused upon Roger. "Why won't she ride in the car with you?"

Roger stumbled over his words as he attempted an explanation, his voice trailing without clearly answering the question. Even though he rephrased the question, Roger's response continued to be ambiguous. Roger glanced my way. Emotions flooded over me. Anger, embarrassment, shame, and something else. Disgust? How do I clearly identify all those feelings? Feelings directed inwardly, as well as toward my husband. I wished I had not self-disclosed the dysfunctional relationship between father and daughter, let alone between Roger and myself, but once words are said they can't be snatched back.

So, I pushed the emotions aside, tucking them away in a little cubicle in the darkest recesses of my mind. They would make their way out again, but today was not the day. Straightening my spine, I made eye contact with this man who appeared sincere in his offer to help and attempted to explain.

"Sarah and her father have a poor relationship. He has been emotionally and physically abusive to Sarah. We have received counseling, but Sarah refuses to be in a confined space with him."

He paused as he processed this revelation. He glanced at Roger, who looked away. He focused his attention on me.

"How old is Sarah?"

"She is thirty."

"Does she pay rent?"

"No."

"Why is she living in your home, especially considering the history?"

"It's complicated. She only recently moved back after her boyfriend overdosed and died. She needed our support."

I omitted the fact that her boyfriend had overdosed in our driveway in the middle of the night several weeks earlier. This conversation was not easy but pushing through it was paramount to giving us some sort of hope, hope that it was not too late for Sarah... or for us.

His message was clear as he handed me several of his business cards.

"Give her an ultimatum. Set a date for her to either accept treatment or leave your home. It is my hope that this will reinforce to her that you are serious and provide motivation for her to engage in the process of seeking and accepting appropriate treatment. Each day, give her one of my cards and urge her to call me. Then leave it alone."

He focused again on Roger. "You probably should stay out of this conversation at this point, considering the history between you and Sarah. Unfortunately, your wife will need to have this conversation with your daughter. That does not mean you cannot be supportive of your wife. She is going to need all the support you can give her. Do you understand?"

Roger remained silent but shook his head affirmatively.

This older man has faced his own family battles. He has wisdom. Experience. What he says must be true. Right? His stern admonition to be firm with Sarah hit me as he looked directly at me—our eyes locked. We were battling for Sarah's life. He knew it. I knew it. Did Roger fully recognize his daughter's life lay in the balance? He must.

They slowly walked us out of the small office into the hallway. They smiled and shook our hands, wishing us good luck. We were going to need more than luck. We needed a miracle.

A police detective, perhaps in his forties walked to the car with us.

He was tall, slim, mustached, wearing a suit, a white shirt and a tie. His dark brown hair grazed his shirt collar. No smiles from him. All business. He followed us out to the car where we left the pills and drug paraphernalia I had found in Sarah's room, confiscated and brought with us today.

I opened the hatchback and reached in to grab a simple, unassuming white plastic grocery bag. Inside are drugs, brown capsules of unknown etiology kept in little brown bags. Needles and syringes. He took the bag without a word, turned away and walked back into the jail.

As I closed the hatchback, I let out a breath of relief that we have released them to proper authorities who will analyze them and let us know exactly what we were dealing with; not considering how easily Sarah was able to replace them. The most important thing I should have given them, but forgotten, was the spoon with just a tiny bit of drug residue left on its inner surface, which I had hidden, months later to be found, causing the grief and anxiety to bob to the surface, opening the healing wound, a scab ruthlessly torn away.

We pulled out of the parking lot heading for home that unusually warm November afternoon. I turned my gaze to take in the intensely blue skies and white puffy clouds. The tires hummed on the asphalt. Roger looked straight ahead. We were silent, lost in our thoughts. Does he have regrets? I do.

A beautifully mild day for late fall, but I am cold. My hands are ice. My heart squeezes with the knowledge of what I must do—confrontation. With Sarah. No more denial. Blinders removed. Is it too late? Why must I do this alone? If only it could be the two of us as a team; two parents expressing love and concern sitting down to offer unconditional support to our deeply troubled daughter. Strength. I must find the strength. No choice really. Her life was in the balance, and I feared this was too little...far too late.

ULTIMATUM

"IF I HAD KNOWN THIS WAS MY AUNT'S LAST THANKSGIVING WITH US, I WOULD NOT HAVE LET HER LEAVE..."

This day when families celebrate Thanksgiving, I must give my daughter an ultimatum—two weeks to agree to treatment. She stood by the front door to say goodbye, her LL Bean pink duffle bag by her side. She comes and goes like a ghost. Up and down the stairway, silent, careful, secretive. This time, I am more aware, and stopped her before she left. There is something important I must say to her. No more holding back, afraid. Afraid of what? What does it matter now?

Before she could walk out the door, I asked, "Sarah, it looks like you're about to leave. Where are you going?"

"I'm going to spend Thanksgiving with Heather and the kids."

"Oh, that's good. Please give them my love?"

"I will."

"Before you leave, can we talk for a minute?"

"Mom, why do you pick the time to talk just as I'm leaving?"

How do I respond to that? How do I explain that what I need to say cannot wait? Do I reveal to her that if I do not say this now, I will never say it and I will regret it for the rest of my life? How do I say if we do not have this conversation now, there may never be another opportunity to have it?

Instead, I walked up to her and hugged her tightly. Her arms encircled me. The connection was broken all too soon as we stepped away. Somehow, I needed to find the strength to speak frankly. No mincing words. No affectation. First, I needed to reaffirm my love, the most important thing of all.

"Sarah, I love you so much. What I need to say is important. I'm saying this because I love you with all of my heart."

My voice catches. I am close to tears.

Her voice is barely a whisper.

"I love you too, Mom."

I gazed directly into her eyes. I held out my hand in supplication towards her.

"I can't let you leave today until I make something very clear. We are here for you and will do everything in our power to support and help you. We have found treatment options for you and it will cost you nothing."

"We? Who is we? There is no we," she interjected forcefully.

This time I ignored her and continued.

"You and I both realize you are sick and need treatment right away. You have two weeks to make a choice. Either you begin treatment for your addiction or you need to leave our home. We simply can't keep going on like this."

Stricken, she said, "So, you're kicking me out. I knew that's what you'd do."

"Sarah, we are not abandoning you. We are not kicking you out. You need help. Please, think about this and let me know your decision."

But in reality, isn't that exactly what was happening? Tough love. Either she does what we want her to (even though what we wanted could be a life-saving choice) or she could no longer stay under our roof. In her altered state of mind, she was hearing, feeling judgment and rejection.

Her argument up to now had been that treatment would be too expensive and she had no insurance. She could not argue that now. Sadness and fear flashed across her face. Perhaps something more. Shame? The stigma of addiction is paralyzing. Her eyes were wide reflecting shock and hurt, but she remained silent. I watched in my own silence, engulfed in fear and worry as she turned away, brushing away her own tears. She realized that her long-kept secret was a secret no more. My disclosure reaffirmed to her that I cannot live with the fear of losing her.

Tears streamed down my cheeks as I reached out to grip her hands in mine. Her beautiful hazel eyes widened, filled with unimaginable suffering as she stared into my own.

"Please, don't do this to me. I do not want to be the one to find you. The next time this happens, I may find you too late. It will kill me."

A single tear fell from her eye as she whispered, "I'm sorry mom."

She turned away and walked out the door.

Sarah was off to her sister's place to spend Thanksgiving. Their home, unlike ours, would be far from silent. Messy, chaotic. A home filled to the brim with seven children, two dogs and a cat or two. Laughter. Squabbling. Love. We do not celebrate this holiday as a family. Jehovah's Witnesses do not celebrate holidays.

Even though I no longer practiced this faith, my husband continued to be deeply involved. A few weeks ago, I bought a turkey and put it in the freezer, but what is the point? Sarah's older sister, Sherry had invited us to eat Thanksgiving dinner with them. Her dad refused, but I will go. For me, being with family during this stressful time is paramount. Being with others to laugh, converse and share our love is my need; not sitting across from a man who I have lost connection to.

Much later, after Sarah's death, her thirteen-year-old niece, Tierra plaintively posted on Facebook something heart-wrenching.

"If I had known this was my aunt's last Thanksgiving with us, I would not have let her leave..."

Sarah confided with her sister, Heather that weekend that I was kicking her out. That was not my intended message. What she heard and what I said somehow crossed the divide of communication to become words of rejection rather than words offering hope and support.

ACCIDENT

Summer. I am outside about to leave for a walk. It is late in the afternoon, early evening really. The air is balmy and warm. It has been a beautiful sunny August day. A silver Saab pulls into the driveway and stops. The car door opens, and Sarah swings her long, tanned legs out exiting her car. I have not seen her for about a week, and I smile my welcome.

"Hi, Sarah! This is a nice surprise!" She walks toward me, then stops just a few feet away.

"Hi, Mom. Were you about to leave?"

"Just going for a walk. It's great to see you!" We close the distance between us to hug.

"Hey mom, is it just me, or are you getting shorter she teases?"

This seems to be a running joke between her and her brother, Donnie. We always welcome each other with hugs, and each of them need to bend low to do so. He is almost six feet and she is only a couple inches shorter.

Laughing, I step away and look up into my daughter's lovely face. Her face seems thinner. I look more closely noticing tape residue on her arms and upper chest. She is wearing blue shorts and her favorite peach-colored tank top, accentuating her summer tan. Brown LL

Bean flip-flops clad her feet. Her toenails painted pink. Bruises, yellow and blue, beginning to fade, but still evident, are scattered across her upper arms. Tape residue is on each collarbone. Concern flashes and arcs. I look at her questioningly. “What happened to you? Are you okay?”

“Oh, nothing serious, mom. I was in a small car accident. I’m fine.”

She lies so easily. I accept her words, but niggling doubts lurk in my mind. I want to ask her questions, but her face closes. Her eyes seem to send me a warning. “Not now, Mom.”

Shutters. Secrets. I can read her body language. She is not going to give me more information. I wait. Bide my time. When she is ready to share, she will. Still, I express my concern. “Sarah, I’m worried for you. Are you sure you’re okay?”

“Mom, I’m okay, but I am hungry. What did you have for supper? Do you have any leftovers? Is dad home?

“No, it’s Tuesday night. He’s at his meeting.” A little sigh escapes her.

“Oh, okay. We have the house to ourselves then?”

“Yup, we do.”

My walk forgotten, together, we go into the house. She heads for the kitchen and the refrigerator. She is not too keen on using the microwave though.

“Mom, the microwave is not healthy. It gives off radiation you know. You really shouldn’t use it.”

Instead, she warms the leftovers on the gas stove. She places the food on a plate and together we sit at the kitchen table to make small talk while she eats. I cannot help but glance at her bruises and the tape residue. She notices. “Mom, I’m okay. No worries.” She flashes a smile. Call it mother’s intuition, but I sense not all is as it seems. She is not fine.

After eating, she goes up to her room for a while. Later, she quietly descends the stairs and pauses by the door to say goodbye, her pink duffle bag slung over her shoulder.

Disappointed in her brief visit I ask, “Leaving so soon?”

"Yup. Thanks for feeding me! Love you! See you soon."

We hug goodbye. I stand on the deck to watch her as she strides quickly toward her car, opens its door, climbs behind the wheel and starts the engine. She looks up to give me a quick wave goodbye. I raise my hand, returning the gesture. She backs out into the road and drives away. My hand drops to my side.

The evening is beginning to settle in. Twilight. Birdsong. A gray squirrel, chattering scurries up the chestnut tree. Leaves rustle in the cool evening breeze. I turn back toward the house to walk inside. Sarah's cat, Boo-Boo runs up the steps and arcs his back, rubbing against my legs, his fur soft and silky. I open the door, he scoots inside, running for his food dish. I scoop out a bit of wet cat food and drop it in his dish. He eats happily, purring. Roger will be home soon. I tidy up the kitchen. A niggle of worry lingers, a tingle of something...fear? Concern? What?

~

SUMMER, SUN & WATER

Two weeks pass before I see Sarah again. She has been gone most of the summer, camping out with her current love in the front yard of his parents' home.

His parents live in a small coastal town that offers tourists a taste of Maine's beautiful coastline in the summer. Scores of hotels dot the landscape as the colorful sails of boats cruise the bay. Out of state visitors, enticed by an eclectic mix of activities such as whale watching, deep-sea fishing, sailing, and sunset tours off the rocky coast of Maine fill the shops and streets.

The town thrives, swelling with humanity during the summer as the local restaurants offer scintillating Maine seafood and lobster. People from all over the country fill this little town to bursting. The tourist shops do well. Sarah has snagged a job at a hotel and her boyfriend is working at a nearby marina. His parents are overjoyed that he has found a job. They reveal to Sarah that he has not worked a regular job for a long time. They think Sarah is the catalyst. That she is good for him. "A good influence," were her words. Sarah smiled as she shared this bit of info—a smile that somehow never reached her eyes. I wondered.

The two are in love. When not working, the two of them picnic at the beach. He takes her picture with her back turned. The sunset is her backdrop, pink, lavender, deep purple and blue swirl in a kaleidoscope of colors embracing Sarah's form. Wearing her favorite wrap, colorful and translucent, it flutters behind her as the seaside breeze lifts it, surrounding her hallow-like. Its colors of red, gold and green flutters, dances, kite-like, around her. She is wearing a two-piece swimsuit, the top black and the bottom pink as she plays in the surf. She is beautiful. The ocean, flashing bits of light, shimmers as she wades at the edge.

A summer of self-discovery. Friendship deepening into love. When I see her, she glows! She is also fearful. "I'm scared, mom. I'm falling for him, and I don't want to hurt him."

You have been in and out of relationships for years now. This is your thirtieth summer. You have been searching for someone who would love you unconditionally, not just for the sex. You have been longing for someone who loves your intellect and your humor; someone who understands all the intricacies of your personality, needs, and desires. Is he the one? Until now, you have been terribly disillusioned and mistreated.

She confides, "He makes me feel so good about myself, mom. He wakes me in the morning with butterfly kisses. He makes me laugh when I am sad. He makes jokes that change my mood from darkness to the light. He laughs at my insecurities and tells me I can accomplish anything. He said that together we could build a life. I think he is the one. No one, of all the men I've known, has made me feel like this, mom."

Sarah sits at the table talking while in the basement the washing machine agitates and the dryer whirls away. She is waiting for her laundry to finish. We drink iced beverages and make salad while she shares her hopes and her fears about this newly budding relationship. I listen, smile, and try to make all the appropriate responses, as images of a hopeful future for her form in my mind.

Beneath her revelations of love, a dark side lurked. I did not want to know. I did not want to recognize that they shared a deeper connection, more than just a growing attraction toward each other. I did not want to know about the drug use, the partying, and the drug connections they both had developed over the years.

When she introduced him to me, I observed a young man with long, twisted dreadlocks. He was slight of frame with deeply fringed brown eyes. His smile was sweet, almost wistful. He was respectful and considerate of her. His speech was intriguing with a slight burr. I tried to define it.

He was courteous and presented himself with an aura that oozed kindness. What impressed me was how his eyes followed her, reading her cues and responding positively. He doted on her. They worked as one; Sarah gathered as he deftly and quickly chopped vegetables for a salad. I watched and listened with rapt attention.

"Eating healthy is important. When are you going to start a compost pile, Mom? I am glad you are getting your veggies from the farm. Organic is the way to go."

A running commentary. He would bob his head and laugh as she rambled on, flashing smiles of approval at her. Her face flushed. Her hazel eyes happy. She seemed to be losing weight but appeared healthy.

I wanted to believe all was good. I wanted to look into his heart, and not judge him for his nonchalant hippy-like appearance. He reminded me of the character in the Disney Movie, Pirates of the Caribbean. He looked startlingly like a benevolent Captain Jack Sparrow. His description was colorful and romantic. "A person of equally dubious morality and sobriety…who fights a constant and losing battle with his own best tendencies."

However, he was not a benevolent Jack Sparrow. He was a man on the brink of disaster, skirting it for years. He was a man hearing voices, a man with a long-standing history of drug use and exploration. A man who my daughter believed she loved.

CRASH

JUST LIKE THAT, SUDDENLY YOUR WORLD CRASHED AND BURNED...

Early September 2016

Sarah comes home in the wee hours of the morning to do laundry. I do not hear her, but her father does. I am sleeping in the upstairs bedroom across the hall from hers. Her dad sleeps downstairs. He uses a C-Pap machine for his sleep apnea, which disrupts my sleep. He is aware of her entering the home while I sleep soundly. She is downstairs in the basement feeding her clothes to the washing machine. It takes her longer than usual because she left a receipt or tissue in a pocket and she is picking tiny pieces of shredded paper off the clothes. Sarah articulated these events in her journal; words I found after she had died. The date she wrote these words: a mere eleven days before her death.

November 5, 2016,

"Why the fuck didn't you follow through on getting our laundry washed at the laundromat in town so I'm not coming home for it—you always said it was fine but affording it was always a problem? So, I would love to blame you for everything, but I feel so guilty. I shouldn't have left you for so long wasting time shaking little bits of paper off clothes since I forgot a receipt in my pocket or something and tiny bits covered several items. I'm shaking

them out, cursing, and you're in the car—going through an overdose that claimed the love I finally found, looked forward to everyday, made me smile. I found a man who truly saw all of me and celebrated me for it. My faults were poked fun at while being addressed in a sensitive, caring, and loving way."

Tragedy struck soundlessly with no warning. I had no premonition or ominous feelings. I learned later that she and her boyfriend had been arguing. He stayed in the car while she took her laundry into the house and downstairs to the basement. Sarah's words continued. Reading them enlightened me. Reading them broke my heart all over again.

"I feel like I led you astray. We held hands and my negative pieces took hold—in stress, in happiness, just for the hell of it. I didn't need any reason. Wish I never dragged you through my shit. I knew that I was/am weak towards this shit. Severely crippling, life-altering, negative consequences and you just wanted to make me happy. I knew you liked to have your fun too, but you knew your tolerance was low. You knew this shit was good. And me? I didn't talk our argument out. Maybe things would have been different—we would have stayed talking and you would have never been left alone..."

While she tends to her laundry, he makes a conscious decision as he reaches into the backpack. Heroin. He uses. Supposedly he has not used for a long time. Is that the truth? Perhaps. Who knows the truth? I certainly do not, but this time was his last. He began to overdose in the car, which they had parked in our driveway. When Sarah went out to the car to talk to him, she found him. Frantic and fearful, she called 911.

I did not hear any sirens. Flashing blue lights did not awaken me. They came in the darkness of night. Men in dark clothing and badges.

Did she implore, "Don't wake my parents?"

Did they glance toward our darkened home, and then back toward her stricken face? Secrets.

They scooped his inert form onto a stretcher, placed him quickly into the box-like emergency vehicle, and silently drove away.

I did not know any of this until later the next day when her eldest sister, Sherry called me. The ambulance transported him to the hospital in the town Sherry lived in, thirty miles away, rather than to the local hospital nearest us.

Overwhelmed, exhausted and nearly incoherent, Sarah knocked on her sister's door later that day as she gasped, "I need you."

She fell into her sister's arms sobbing. Eventually, Sarah was able to communicate what had happened. Spent emotionally and physically after drinking her sister's wine and eating only a little, Sarah fell asleep.

Sherry called to fill me in while Sarah slept. Her voice was low.

"Mom, Sarah is here. Her boyfriend overdosed last night. He is in the hospital. Things do not look good for him. He's in a coma. Sarah is sleeping now so I thought this would be a good time to call you. She is in a bad state mom. I am not sure what to do. If she will let us, we will drive her home, but she is stubborn, and she does not even have her own car. I'm not sure whose car it is."

We talked as Sherry gave me as many details as she could. I am dazed when she reveals where this all happened. In our own driveway, early this morning as we slept. Just a few hours before the sun would rise to welcome the sound of birds singing as the early morning mist rose from the grass and fields.

When Sarah woke up, she refused her sister's offer to drive her home. Sherry called me after Sarah left to tell me, "She's on her way home, mom."

What do I say to Sarah when she walks in? Is any family ever prepared to deal with tragedy? I offer only what I know. Love. Support. A long hug. A listening ear as she reveals her waking nightmare.

Sarah described the scene vividly. "His parents came to the hospital. His mom screamed at me and told me it was my fault. She said I didn't belong there and to leave."

She described how her husband hung back, silent, in the background, not saying a word, allowing his ex-wife to verbally assault her. His apparent fear of this woman, once his wife seemed clearly evident. Reticent, culled and meek, while his wife, consumed with rage, was explosive, volatile.

"Mom, I don't understand. He told me this summer he loved me as a daughter and he was happy that his son and I were together." Her tears fall, her face twists, crumbles as she continues. I listen silently, reaching for her hand.

Sherry later fills me in more fully. Appalled at the scene unfolding before her, never meeting this family before, she was unsure how to respond. "Mom, that woman was verbally assaultive. I think she was on the verge of attacking Sarah physically. I could not just stand there and not defend Sarah. I tried to deescalate a situation that appeared to be building into a possible physical assault."

"What did you say to her," Sherry?

I told her, "I understand how horrible this is for you. We will leave. We only want to show respect for your family and what you're going through but cursing and attacking my sister is unacceptable and inappropriate, and I won't stand for it."

As Sherry turned away with the intent to leave, Sarah, torn and conflicted, still stood near her boyfriend's hospital door. A young woman of about eighteen walked out of his hospital room and saw Sarah. She turned toward the raging woman telling her, "I'll talk to Sarah, Grams. I'll take care of this."

The three of them walked to the cafeteria. Sitting down, cups of coffee slowly cooling in front of them, she implored Sarah to give up their secrets.

"If you know where my dad got the drugs, please tell me. We need to know."

Sarah, opened her mouth, but then closed it tightly. "I'm sorry, but I can't tell you. I want to tell you, but I just cannot. I'm sorry."

Her face is a mask as she asks, "You can't, or you won't?"

Sarah lowers her eyes in despair. "I can't. I just can't."

Sherry observes anguish and fear in Sarah's voice, and tried to reason with her as well.

"Sarah, if you know please tell her. The family needs closure. It's their right to know what happened. He is her dad."

Sarah refuses to be forthcoming. "I'm so sorry, but I can't tell you."

"Then, you need to leave," she told Sarah.

Sarah began to sob uncontrollably. Sherry put her arms around her as they both rose from their chairs and left the hospital.

Even though his family did not want Sarah there, she went every day to visit him. Later she shared with me some of which she said to him as she held his hand.

Scared and full of remorse, she implored him. "I know you can hear me. I love you. Please do not leave me. Squeeze my hand if you can hear me."

Every day, when his family had gone, she approached his room to be at his bedside. Near the end of the week, as she held his hand and talked to him, she believed she saw his eyes flicker. She was certain that she felt his hand lightly squeeze her own. She immediately told the nurse her observations. His family was coming soon though, so she had to leave. It. Nearly a week had passed.

The next day, she learned that his family signed the papers, permitting removal of their son from life support. The machines that forced air into his lungs keeping his body alive were unplugged. According to attending physicians, his brain was no longer viable. Braindead.

"Mom, he was recovering. Why couldn't they wait just a little longer? Why would they do that?" She sobbed in my arms her grief. It was a blow to her. Her guilt and remorse consumed her.

~

GRIEF & THREATS

Days passed as Sarah slowly became a shadow. In her room day and night, the window covered, the room darkened. She left the house briefly and intermittently, only returning to ascend the stairs to her room. Occasionally eating. Crying or just staring at the wall curled into a ball. One night, I paused by her door. It was partially open, and she was on her computer. She was crying. Opening the door, I walked into her room and asked, "Sarah, I'm so sorry. What can I do? I want to help."

"Nothing. There's nothing you can do."

I learned later through Sarah's sister, Heather that Sarah was receiving threatening messages from her boyfriend's family.

"Why don't you die, bitch?" Just do it; kill yourself, bitch. We HATE you. You should have died, not him. DIE YOU FUCKING BITCH."

Several times a day I would knock on her door offering food, comfort. Her response, "Go away. I'm not hungry." Sometimes I did, but other times I simply could not leave her, but went in anyways to sit on her bed for a moment. Repeatedly she turned her back to me. I would touch her shoulder. She would shrug me away. I would leave her room but was never far from her side; hovering, listening, watching. Fear and worry hovered over me like a dark cloud.

REACHING OUT

Distraught and wild with worry, I made an appointment with my family doctor. Tearfully, I confided in her.

"There is someone here who may be able to help. She is care manager for the health center, a social worker. She knows Sarah. Sarah has spoken with her before. She is skilled with challenges such as this. Perhaps Ellen can reach her."

She walked me down the hallway, into the waiting area, through another wing, then to the end of the hallway. She knocked on Ellen's office door. A woman, young enough to be my daughter greeted us with a warm smile. Dr. Hamilton introduced me, briefly explaining my concerns.

Really though, how can she truly explain what I am feeling? Fear. Anguish. Sadness. Worry. Oh, my God, so much worry. Ellen and I talked for almost an hour in-between my tears. She was silent, allowing me to express my emotions, then regain composure. I understood what she was doing. Silence allows many things.

Ellen was kind, soft-spoken. She asked a few questions. She admitted to meeting with Sarah in the past but offered no more. Ellen tried to console me and offered to see Sarah, giving me her business card.

I glanced at her card then at her face, into her warm brown eyes. "Sarah has been less than cooperative. I am at a loss here. I will tell her that I spoke with you and that you are willing to talk to her."

"Tell her that there are options and if she will just come in to talk to me we can figure out things. It is possible to overcome insurance issues. At this point, that is the least of our worries. In the meantime, I will make some calls and see what we can come up with from my end. I am here if you need me. I will check in with you and Sarah in a bit. It that okay?"

"Thank you. Yes, that will be fine."

Ellen offers me her hand and she squeezed mine in a kind way. Leaving the office, I allowed myself to feel hope. I cannot give up hope. Without it, well...I just do not know.

HOPELESSNESS

Home now. Sarah was still in her room. I reached into my pocket and felt Ellen's business card. Lunch. Yes, I will make lunch. A sandwich on a plate, I climbed the stairs to Sarah's room and knocked on her door. I heard her mumbling as I pushed her door open. Sarah sat at her desk, her eyes focused on her laptop. Good, at least she is out of bed. Enlisting a cheerful voice, which she knew was clearly fake, I told her, "I have a sandwich for you."

She glanced my way. Her eyes were red. Her hair hung limply around her shoulders. I am not sure when she last showered. The room was messy and stale. I put the plate on her desk beside her and she croaked, "Thanks, mom, so where have you been? Ah, a spark of curiosity. That is good.

I sat down on the edge of her bed to tell Sarah about my conversation with Ellen. I reached into my pocket, pulled out Ellen's card and placed it on her desk.

Sarah glanced at the card and shook her head. Her voice monotone, her expression flat as she responded.

"I've spoken with her before. There is nothing she can do for me. No one can help me."

I am beginning to believe she is right. Defeated, hopeless, I turned aside and left Sarah's room.

Several days passed. Concerned, Ellen, from the health center, called to check in on Sarah.

"I've been thinking about your family and wanted you to know that I'm here. Is there anything I can do?"

"I honestly do not know! She's grieving heavily and seldom comes out of her room. I am so worried. I've told her that I spoke with you, but at this point, she doesn't want to talk to anyone."

I remembered someone saying, "She has suffered a loss. She is grieving. This is normal."

Was it Dr. Hamilton or Ellen? I just do not remember. Why is it I struggle to believe these words? Ellen is familiar with Sarah's challenges and tried to reassure me. However, her reassurance seemed hollow and rested like bile in my throat. She meant well. I know that, but my reality was this. I was on constant alert, checking on Sarah around the clock. Grief, so deeply felt, kills. I was watching her slowly die.

Days passed, a week. Then one day Sarah simply got out of bed, showered and dressed. She began to eat. She started to smile. She began to talk. I sighed inwardly with relief thinking this was a positive turn. My hope revived. My thoughts? She is going to be okay, now. Right?

Ellen called again to check in with us.

"She seems to be recovering," I told her. The relief in her voice audible as she said, "I'm so glad."

REVELATION

November 2016

Sarah and I were talking in her room. A look of resolve came over her face as she confided the truth.

"Remember when I told you about the accident I had in August?"

I looked at her questioningly as I responded with a tentative, "Yes."

She was having trouble making eye contact at first, but she raised her eyes and I thought I saw fear and…was it perhaps relief?

"Well, it wasn't actually a car accident, but it was an accident. I overdosed. The people I was with called 911 and I was taken to the hospital."

How does a mother respond to such a revelation? I tried not to overreact. In the past, if my reaction was too strong, she would retreat and shut down after opening to me or worse, she would become angry defensively responding, "Why are you giving me a hard time?"

She was parroting behavior much like her father, which I knew would hurt and wound her if I told her so.

The pattern of communication that had developed between Roger and I through the years had become, I now understood as dysfunctional. Often, when voicing a concern or a question with the intent for clarification, his response was defensive. He would appear annoyed, angry. His typical responses?

"What are you complaining about now? What is wrong with you now? Why are you making things so hard?"

I interpreted his inflections, body language and words as an attempt to shut me down, mute me, to induce feelings of guilt, which then invoked self-doubt and inner questioning; *"Did I actually have a valid concern? Was I being difficult and hard to get along with?"*

Not clearly understanding then, that his behavior could be identified as emotional manipulation. Was he attempting to deflect his own insecurities back toward me?

Determined. Ever hopeful things can change, I continued my attempts to reason with him, modeling the words I needed him to use. Repeatedly explaining I deserved to be spoken to kindly, respectfully. I needed his reassurance, not recrimination. I needed so much more than what he seemed able to give.

Despite years of trying, my reasoning continually fell on deaf ears. His behavior seemingly changing for the short-term after a particularly nasty event, but quickly reverting back, causing me to become closed, quiet, unresponsive, cold. Why open my heart when the end result is more often than not hurt and disappointment? Why trust when trust is so quickly broken?

Hence, I recognized the importance of fostering Sarah's openness, and feared she would retreat again if I began (her words) to lecture her.

Pausing, giving myself some time to think of how to respond to this terrifying revelation, I did what had become instinctive. Reaching out, I hugged her to me tightly, and her arms enveloped me as we clung to each other.

We slowly separated. It was my turn to be honest with her now.

"Sarah, I didn't believe you when you told me that day you had been in an accident. I thought there was more to your story."

She looked at me in surprise, and with anguish in her voice she implored, "Why didn't you ask me for the truth then? Don't you care about me?"

Her hurt sliced through me and self-doubt filled my heart.

"Oh, God Sarah. You know I care about you. To be fair, I *did* question you! Do you remember? You reassured me that you were fine. You closed up. You are such a private person and as an adult, I try to respect that. I want you to confide in me when you are ready and feel it's wrong to coerce it out of you."

The accusation in her voice and eyes dissolved, replaced with perception. I sat down on the edge of her bed, turning my face to make eye contact.

Gently, carefully, I responded to her revelation, "Thank you for finally being honest with me. It took courage to tell me. We need to make a plan, don't you think?"

She looked tired. Her dark blonde hair, once thick and wavy had lost its volume and seemed to be thinning. I noticed she has lost more weight. My eyes were seeing her in a new light; the lens previously distorted and murky, now clear. My blinders stripped away.

"Mom, don't worry. I am going to get treatment. I'm researching options."

She wanted to reassure me. I wanted to believe her. She was so convincing.

I asked her, "What are you going to do?"

She responded, "Don't worry about it. I've got this."

That evening, about ten o'clock, on my way to bed, I walked past her room and glanced in. She sat at her desk intently looking at something on her laptop. I paused to say goodnight. For a long time, her sleep had been disturbed. While her family sleeps, she cannot. Restless and anxious, precious sleep eludes her.

She swiveled to look my way.

"Mom, do you have a moment?"

Stressed, tired, and sick with worry, I swallowed it all.

"Sure. What's up?"

"I want to show you something. I have been doing some research and I think I found treatment that will work for me. Will you please have an open mind and watch this with me?"

"Ok. I'll try, Sarah."

I sat down on the bed as she opened a window on her laptop containing a YouTube video. She clicked on the arrow in the middle of the video, inducing a surge of hope as I realized she was researching treatment options for her addiction. I watched intently as the video unfolded, but hope began to fade. The short video promoted a controversial method of treating opioid addiction using high doses of marijuana. Despite the sinking feeling in my gut, I watched it silently, while inwardly my skepticism grew.

Captivated, she watched the video as the light from the screen flickered off her face in the darkened bedroom. It was not a long video, maybe ten minutes or so. When it ended, she turned towards me with expectation and something else. Something I had not heard in her voice for a long time—a bit of hope.

"I'm going to contact him mom. I know him anyway. He is a *caregiver*. I've been to his farm before."

"You have? Where is his farm?" I was unfamiliar with the term *caregiver,* so I asked her, "What is a caregiver?"

Patiently, as though talking to a child, she explained. "A caregiver is someone who grows marijuana legally and provides it for the dispensaries."

I was aware that Maine had recently legalized marijuana for medicinal purposes and there were dispensaries providing it in many towns across the state, including ours.

She continued, "I think it will work and I want to try it."

My mind was racing. How in the world could she think this would work? Adding to my doubt of the effectiveness and futility of this treatment, the video explained that it did not work for everyone. A person who had gone through the treatment was interviewed near the end of the video. He admitted to quickly relapsing and began reusing opioids shortly after completing the treatment.

I shared with her my concerns, observations. Ignoring them, she countered defensively, "I thought you'd be happy that I'm seeking treatment. I do not want to use suboxone or methadone. It is worse than heroin and more addictive. Marijuana is natural and real, not manufactured."

Her reasoning contained validity, but in my mind, it was still flawed. She had been using marijuana since she was a teenager. She had earlier self-disclosed to me that she smoked marijuana daily to ease her anxiety and stress. Though marijuana is legal in Maine, I do not approve its use as a recreational drug. Using it to counter opiate addiction was totally foreign to me and I simply could not wrap my mind around it as an effective method.

Making eye contact I attempted to reason with her, explaining my newfound knowledge. "I've been researching treatment options. Alternative treatment options are available, especially now that you are actively seeking it. Methadone does not need to be a part of it if you don't want to use it."

Her response was quick. Decisive. "Mom, too many people go into detox and as soon as they are released, they relapse. A lot of them die. I have seen it with my own eyes. Many of them were my friends. I do not want to die. I want to try this. I'm going to call him."

Well, I didn't want her to die either! I wanted to be supportive and be open to all forms of alternative treatment, but this one did not make sense to me. I said nothing more. Her attention refocused on the screen, dismissing me. She had been smoking marijuana for years while simultaneously using opioids, developing dependence leading to addiction. How in the world did she think it would help her stop using opioids? I did not understand her mindset. It did not make sense to me. Her altered brain state became more evident to me that night, and I felt powerless to change it.

REALIZATION

The next day, I called the health center again, leaving a message with the nurse to have Dr. Hamilton call me as soon as possible.

Late afternoon, as darkness fell on that cold day in early December, Dr. Hamilton finally got back to me. Exiting the market, my basket filled with groceries, people surrounded me, but I felt so alone. They were oblivious to my pain. The phone to my ear, I asked her to give me just a moment as I loaded the bags of groceries into the van, returning the cart as quickly as I could.

Finally, in the van, the door closed for privacy, I could now speak freely. I knew what I needed to do. I had never dreamed that I would have to make this request. Desperate, knowing Sarah's time with us was running out, I filled Dr. Hamilton in. A brief silence ensued before she responded.

I do not remember exactly what she said, but the gist of her response was this.

"I'm so sorry. If she is determined to go a certain course, there is little we can do."

Defeated. I felt so defeated. Resolute, I made my request. I am a parent, a mom experiencing a waking nightmare; a child addicted.

Again, that hesitation before she responded. Her voice was husky, muted. I sensed her sadness and regret. She knows our family. She is aware of the stressors we have endured. The significant health crises, deaths of loved ones, including my parents and my sister, marital issues. Up to this point, I have somehow found the strength to push through the crises, the losses. Her voice reflected defeat and regret as she said, "Yes, I will do that. At this point, I agree that you should have this on hand, just in case. I'll call it in to your pharmacy."

"Thank you." There was nothing more to say. I ended the call but continued to look at the glowing screen. It was dark in the van except for dim glow from the tall light poles interspersed throughout the store's parking lot. Headlights swept by to reflect their light briefly into the van; cars entered and exited. My cellphone now slept, dark, blank, like my soul. Darkness assaulted me and there seemed to be no light to guide me out and beyond this abysmal feeling of impending doom.

Dr. Hamilton has known Sarah from infancy. She inoculated her against childhood illnesses. Chicken pox, measles, diphtheria, mumps, rubella, polio. She treated her strep throats, ear infections, the occasional colds and flu's. Dr. Hamilton treated Sarah during all the traditional childhood illness and provided all the necessary inoculations, but she could not inoculate her against addiction. Her words stick to me as we ended our brief conversation.

"I'm so sorry. There was something so appealing and wistful about her. I wish I could be of more help. I could not reach her. She was elusive to me."

A Hundred Tears Falling From Heaven

As Sarah reached teenage years and early adulthood, Dr. Hamilton provided birth control. When Sarah developed endometriosis and acute pain, Dr. Hamilton referred her to a specialist, who told Sarah she had an ovarian tumor. He recommended surgery. To control her pain after the procedure she was prescribed something new, just on the market, OxyContin. Who knew her addiction would begin with a simple pain pill? When OxyContin hit the market, pharmaceutical companies did not reveal how addictive the medication was.

If physicians were uninformed, of course patients were as well. I could not recognize signs of addiction because addiction never even entered my mind as a possibility, let alone understanding or recognizing the signs of addiction. So, I was in completely the dark as Sarah began a silent fight against a craving that would eventually destroy her, bringing me to this moment in time.

It was raining, a cold and misty winter rain. Freezing rain was in the forecast for later as the temperatures continued to drop. My windshield blurred with raindrops, a hundred tears falling from heaven. Cold, wet, hopeless, I allowed my own tears to fall. I sat there in my car, in the darkness, silently crying as people scurried around me, rushing into and out of the market, their arms hugging their bags of groceries. How much longer would I have to hug my daughter?

They would all soon head home to their families, make dinner, turn on the TV and watch the news. They would laugh and joke with each other or tell their kids to do their homework. Maybe their teenage boy or girl would angrily complain and slam their bedroom door in frustration because their parent has set limits. All the mundane everyday things that normal families do.

Realization hits. I did not have the luxury to cry. I must be strong. No time to wish that things were different or time for self-recrimination. I dried my tears on a stray napkin, stiff and scratchy. Though I understood how self-defeating negative self-talk was, I could not help myself as my inner voice lashed out towards me. I am a bad mom. I do not deserve softness and understanding. I deserve judgment and punishment. Right? Dr. Hamilton's voice continued to echo, "I'm so sorry." *Me too.*

On the way home, I picked up the prescription from the pharmacy. It was in a plain brown paper bag. I walked out of the store holding a substance that may save my daughter's life. I walked past people I have known for years not acknowledging them or saying a word, in a daze. I walked out to the car, my eyes burning with unshed tears. I was resolved.

Home. Sarah was not. I checked her room. Empty food cartons and dirty dishes littered her small space. The trashcan overflowed with soiled tissues and the remains of uneaten food. Her bed was unmade. Piles of clothes were on the bed and on the floor, some in a laundry basket, some not. I have heard it said that one's living space reflects one's state of mind. There was a time when I would have neatened it up. Not today. I left her room as it was.

The small bag I carried contained something I never dreamed I would need to have in my home! Narcan, otherwise known as naloxone, is a nasal spray. If administered quickly, it can lessen the effects of an opioid overdose, but its effects only last for about half-an-hour. Thirty minutes of time as the moments quietly, impersonally pass. A ticking clock, minute by minute, precious moments while life and death is uncertain, tenuous. Sometimes it does not work at all. The unthinkable becomes one's reality.

Until recently, only advanced paramedics were allowed to administer Narcan. Epidemics force change though. First responders, including police officers, firefighters and basic paramedics carry the drug, and now people like me. In one state librarians have it on hand as people overdose in library bathrooms or on a nearby street. Librarians have become first responders too.

The bag I carried felt light and insignificant. How can something weighing next to nothing prevent an overdose or restore a heart already broken? I read the instructions, and then tucked it in my dresser drawer, hoping I would never need to use it. Knowing in my heart the day was rushing closer when I would.

HEATHER

DECEMBER 1, 2016

Sarah's secret is now family knowledge. I found her close to death, but she is still with us, still alive. Thank you, God! Sarah has a choice. Get help and she will have complete family support. If she refuses, she must leave our home. Tough love. Who is it tougher on, the parents or the child? Wait! Sarah is no longer a child, is she? Does tough love really work? Do positive results come from ultimatums?

Sarah told Heather, her older sister, we were kicking her out in two weeks. Communication via texting had been flying back and forth between Heather and me.

Sisters. They shared blonde hair. They shared a room. They shared secrets. How long have they shared secrets of drug use? I am furiously responding to her texts.

She texts, "Sarah told me you're kicking her out of the house. You gave her two weeks. What the hell? She needs love and support, not rejection!"

Anger welled up, hot, burning. I am furious as I respond, "We aren't rejecting her! "Sarah is addicted to heroin. We found treatment for her, but so far, she refuses it. We are giving her a choice. We do love her!"

I knew I was parroting words. Words recently given to me by a drug abuse counselor. Words meant to stir up action. He told me to be decisive, so I continued the conversation (if one can call texting an effective means of conversing.) "If the family is all on the same page, unified in presenting to Sarah she must get into treatment right away, we may be able to save her. If she doesn't get help immediately we are going to lose her!" My voice breaks.

Heather is firm and resolute. My words had little effect. She stood firm in her mindset as she repeated her earlier statement. "She doesn't need judgment and ultimatums. She needs love, nutritious food and support."

Quickly refuting her, I flung back these words: "No! She needs treatment too. She needs to get away from her triggers and easy access to drugs. We have found a place that provides long-term treatment. A state grant covers the cost. All she needs to do is fill out the paperwork. We will get her there. I have told her that. In the meantime, we have spoken to others who offer interim support and treatment. We need to stick together as a family. If you show your support for this arrangement, she may be more responsive."

The texts stopped. A respite, but the next night she called again. The conversation ensued in earnest as I reiterated how scared I was, telling her decisively that her sister needed addiction treatment. Heather continued to be in denial.

"Mom, she is not addicted. You and dad are not supportive, and your attitudes need to change. The environment there is negative, toxic, and is hurting her. If you and dad treat her with love, she'll be all right."

Frustrated, but still hoping to reason with her I continued the conversation. "It's past that now. We do love her. I love her. We have been supporting her and providing her a safe environment. What has she done with it? She is now overdosing in our own home! I finally realize what we have really been doing is enabling her addiction. She is not safe anywhere! To say that all she needs is love is ludicrous. Loving her means recognizing she is in trouble. Loving her means telling her we will not tolerate her drug seeking behavior. Love means setting limits and letting her know we will help and support her with finding appropriate treatment."

Heather responded angrily, "I'm coming down. You need to come and get me," she demanded.

She had no vehicle and lived an hour north of us. Dazed, I asked her, "Tonight? Right now?"

"Yes, tonight, because Sarah needs my support and she's obviously not getting it from you and dad."

I paused for a moment, processing her demand, trying to figure out how to respond. "If I understand correctly you don't agree that she needs to get treatment, right?"

"Look, if you can't be supportive of Sarah's needs right now, then I need to be there to help her sort through all this. I'll take care of her since you obviously can't, and we all know exactly where dad is in the picture."

Wanting to present a unified front between her dad and myself, I told her, "Your dad agrees that she needs treatment too. He's just as scared and concerned as I am." Hoping to help her see reason, I pose an obvious question. "What about the kids?"

She responded quickly, urgently. "My sister is more important right now. They will manage. Come and get me or I'll start hitchhiking."

"If you are coming to encourage her to get into treatment, then we'll get you down here," I told her.

"Look, she doesn't need treatment. She needs love and a lot of care. You are obviously neglecting her."

A host of emotions flooded over me; anger, disbelief, fear. I was temporarily speechless as I processed Heather's demand. I paused because I did not want to say something I could never take back. Finally finding my voice I stated firmly, "No, I'm not coming up there, especially tonight. It is too late. We are exhausted. More importantly, I am not bringing you down here unless your intentions are to be supportive in encouraging her to get into treatment. We do not need more stress here; there is enough of that. We are dealing with her life. If you're not on the same page, then there's no point in continuing this conversation."

Silence and dead space. I kept the connection open waiting for a response, hoping that she finally gets it. Silence.

"Are you still there?" Silence. Silence. The line had gone dead. She was gone. Later, she told me she thought I had hung up on her.

CONFRONTATION

DECEMBER 2, 2016

The next day. Eight p.m. Roger and I drove into the yard after attending a party for friends who were moving out of state. It had been a pleasant evening. Friends, music, food, laughter, dancing. A night allowing us to put aside, if just for a few hours, our fear and worry.

As we parked the car and looked towards the house, we saw that the lights were on. A figure passed by the living room windows. Sarah's car was not in the yard. Who is in the house? I checked the door finding it unlocked. As I pushed open the door, loud music filled the air, its beat angry and assaultive. A female voice, husky and raw was singing loudly to the beat of the music. The smell of coffee and just a hint of tobacco smoke greeted us. I called out, "Is that you, Heather?"

The loud music became softer, less harsh. I watched my daughter; third in the birth tree descend the stairs. She was so thin. She had pulled her long dark blonde hair into a bun, her gauntness accentuated. Her face was pale, stressed. Her ice blue eyes blazed with anger. I read her body language like a book. I knew the signs. She plopped down onto the couch, her arms crossed over her chest.

At the age of thirty-two, she is a woman with huge responsibilities. She has a disabled husband who has brought two of his three children into the family. A blended family. Seven children aged eight through nineteen. A household of nine people crowded into a smallish apartment. Stress etched across the angular lines of her face. My heart constricts because I am powerless against her life choices.

I inhaled slowly to release the tension building inside of me, then glanced at Roger. He sat in his usual spot, the loveseat facing the TV. His eyes shifted away. Great, no help there. Accusations began to fly. Heather was in a manic high of emotion, full of anger and spite but behind her words, I sensed fear. I understood fear. Trying to focus on what was behind the words, and not the words themselves, I steeled myself. Heather's verbal assault began.

"How could you just throw her out? What is wrong with you two? She needs love and support, not judgement and rejection. This house is so full of negativity. No wonder she uses substances. This place is toxic. You two need to make some changes if you want to help her. I would never treat one of my own kids this way."

My own thoughts remained silent, but they spoke loudly in my head. I hoped to God that she would never experience the hell we were going through. She continued with the on-slot. A flood of words. Blaming. Hurtful. Thrusting them with sword-like speed, swiping, cutting, shredding. Anger rose in my chest, tight, constricting as I told myself to breathe—just breathe. I inhaled deeply before responding. Once spoken you can never snatch those words back. I needed to measure them carefully. Never lowering my gaze, maintaining eye contact, I asked her, "What are you doing here, Heather? Are you here to be supportive and encourage Sarah to get into treatment?

She looked at me askance, then scoffed. Anger rose quickly and hotly as I flung at her my own words. "Since it's obvious you aren't and have no intention of helping, you can't stay."

I knew she had no car, no way to leave, unless Sarah took her back home. Where is Sarah anyway? I believed this was all a ploy, worked up by the two of them. Some things never change. Sarah left her sister here to fight her battle for her, pitting her sister against her parents, feeding her half-truths and embellished information. The years leading up to this night seemed to rush up to greet me, as I wondered how in the world we had gotten to this point.

Heather had been articulate and often oppositional in her teen years. Her attitude clearly stated, "I don't give a damn what you think; I'm going to do it anyway."

Sarah followed more quietly and resolutely, forging ahead with her choices, knowing we would not approve. She had developed a life we knew little about. She would nod her head pretending to agree, keeping the waters as smooth as she could. Never one to make ripples. All the while keeping her silence and her secrets as she quietly left, seeking love and acceptance from those eager to use and abuse an innocent. An innocent who quickly lost…everything.

The past swirled away and the present stared starkly. Heather sat defiantly in front of us, in our home, uninvited, telling us in a voice dripping acid, "I'm not going anywhere. I'm here for my sister, not the two of you." She abruptly stood as she snapped, "I need a minute." She grabbed her coffee cup, half-full of cooling coffee, reached for her cigarettes and made her way out the door, slamming it behind her. Cold air swept in, enveloping, chilling.

The door did not latch, so I got up to close it tightly. Anger, red and swelling surged upward and outward. I flung open the door watching her angry strides as she stomped away from the house. Bitterness burned like bile in my throat and words burst from me in a flood. The cold wind swirled around them, sweeping them away, apparently unheard by my daughter's retreating form. She never acknowledged them. I hung my head in regret.

Thus, began seven days of hot and cold, escalating and de-escalating moods, worry, and finally resolution, acceptance and grief, intense, sharp, and undeniable.

Sarah showed up later in the evening. Sisters. One on the brink of death. The other terrified that she was losing her sister, but unable or unwilling to vocalize it, let alone admit the truth to herself, at least not yet.

~

LIES & SECRETS

DECEMBER 3, 2016

It remains unusually warm for Maine, despite being early December. The week ahead offers chilly, fall-like temperatures, but today the sun shines brilliantly, the skies so deeply blue I could lose myself in its vastness. I imagined myself floating high above, looking downward, but removed, unaffected by the turmoil below. An omen of hope? I heard Heather and Sarah talking late into the night. Sisters. Laughter. It was good to hear laughter. It was good to hear music. So much better than silence.

Heather resurfaced from her own darkness the next day to say, "I'm sorry, I misunderstood. She told me the truth. She needs me. I need her. I need to stay for a while. If I stay for a while, maybe I can help her through this."

Four adults under one roof, each with their own agenda, each responding to the crisis differently. My husband retreats into silence and the TV. That damned TV. Watching *Law & Order*, old westerns, the news and current events featuring the opioid epidemic in Maine.

Sarah and Heather have gone out. Gathering my courage, I faced Roger as he sat on the loveseat. Loveseat? Whoever named that piece of furniture that? There is no love in that seat. No, none whatsoever. Turning off the TV, I said, "We need to talk."

He faced me, annoyed. "What's the matter now?" My words came in a rush. So much fear, bitterness and anger.

"We're losing her. She does not feel you love her. She needs you to show and tell her that you do." These words are not new—words articulated many times throughout the years. Somehow, I hoped that if I tried just one more time…

I continue, "You need to get up off that couch and greet her when she comes in the door. You need to sincerely smile and stop saying those annoying insincere words, "How ya doing Sarah?"

He shook his head negatively, "You know that I'm in a lot of pain; my knees are really bad. It's hard to get off the couch."

All I heard were excuses. Eternal excuses for his neglect. Always about him; his pain, his discomfort. Isn't being a parent about making sacrifices? Opening oneself, embracing the role, rather than making excuses why you cannot?

He has always been available to the friends within the Christian congregation. Why is it he could not be that available to his own family? What caused him to close himself off emotionally? How could he so easily express irritation, annoyance, sarcasm with his family, yet express kindness and compassion to those outside of his family? His opportunity to rectify things was running out. Was it already too late?

"Well, you don't seem to have too much trouble getting off it when you want something, do you? If you're hungry or thirsty, or need to go to the bathroom, or Boo-Boo needs to be let in or out, or you decide you want to use the computer, you get up then, don't you?" He does not respond.

I continued, "She's our daughter! We are in crisis; she is in crisis. If ever there was a need for you to take a sincere and active interest in her, this is it. Maybe it is not too late. Emotionally, she is a lost little girl. She needs her father. She has always needed you. Where are you? Where have you been?"

I do not recall everything the two of us said that night. My words rushed out of me forcefully, shoved out by fear so intense it hurt. Time was running out. I was so scared, so damned scared, but even more than that, I was furious…with him. We were in a tennis match volleying words back and forth toward each other. I refused to back down. I volleyed the ball at him with force. My threat was clear as I vehemently threw it at him, "If she dies feeling like you don't give a damn about her, this marriage is dead. You will be dead to me too. Our marriage has been dying for a long time anyway."

His eyes widened—his expression stricken. Just then, Sarah and Heather walked through the door. The two glanced at our faces, knowing their parents had just had words—the energy in the room was charged, our anger, fear and despair no doubt etched on our faces. Sarah walked past her father heading toward the refrigerator to get some water.

As she drank deeply, he found his words. "Sarah, I need your help."

She turned toward him, confused at his unusual request and asked, "What?"

Roger repeated, "I need your help, would you please help me off the couch?"

Heather and I watched Sarah's face, as a host of expressions flickered across it. Confusion, annoyance, a bit of anger, resignation, obligation. He was her dad after all, and he asked her for help. She walked over and extended her hand to help him off the couch. Once he was up, he suddenly wrapped his arms around her. Sarah stood there stiffly in shock as he awkwardly uttered, "I love you. I love you so much."

He continued to embrace her. Tears streamed down his face. We seldom have seen him express intense emotion that included tears. Heather and I froze. What was happening? Heather's shock changed to joy as she rushed over and hugged the two of them. She called out, "Group hug!"

I stumbled across the room to join this once in a lifetime family embrace. Group hug. We were all crying. Sarah's arms raised and wrapped loosely around her dad's frame too, just for a moment. This moment of solidarity, an expression of love, that included their dad, has never happened before, ever! Later, Heather confided, "Mom, Sarah is in the bathroom upstairs. She is crying. She is very confused. What just happened?"

Burying the fear, guilt, and burning anxiety of a family broken. Watching, listening, I try to engage with my damaged daughters. Heather spends as much time as she can with Sarah. Sarah tries to escape.

Her addiction is unrelenting; we do not understand the craving she is experiencing. We do not realize if she does not use she will experience intensely painful withdrawal symptoms. Our knowledge is so limited! She must break away from Heather to buy that tiny packet, a drug that provides a moment of euphoria, falsely offering temporary escape from her inner pain. She finds a place that seems relatively safe —a parking lot. Still in her car, she uses. Then she returns home, seemingly calm, normal. Normal?

The stress continued to build becoming so intense, we must have release. Heather and I took walks attempting to reconnect while Sarah slept. We obtained an uneasy bond again, as we talked about everything under the sun. We laughed with each other, hugged each other and…cried together. One day, as we walked the rail trail, we sat on a boulder facing the river watching an eagle as it dipped and soared in the currents of air above us. The sky brilliantly blue, cloudless. The trees bare, the air crisp. A fish leapt in the water and we watched as the eagle swooped toward the river with amazing speed. Just as quickly this bird of prey rose toward the heavens, a fish in its talons.

A long-time friend, herself Native American, once told me that Native Americans believe rivers are sacred—the giver of life. My daughter's life is uncertain, hanging like frayed, loose thread. As her mother—I gave her life. Can I restore her brokenness, or at the least find those who can? Can I save her?

My musings dissolved as the sound of voices—strangers had appeared on the trail and quickly passed behind us, their voices and laughter fading as their forms disappeared around a corner in the trail. The sun was dipping towards the horizon. Time to leave.

These moments of reconnection for Heather and I were all too fleeting, quickly passing. The hours, the days were speeding away from us. We needed to return home to face the demon that was consuming Sarah.

Heather is intent on sticking as close as she can to her sister's side. It is harder to seek out drugs when your sister is in your space, in your room, in your car, in your business. Somehow, Sarah managed.

I shared what was happening with Donnie. We were in a coffee shop. His response?

"Mom, you are still in the dark. Open your eyes. Heather is sticking close so that when Sarah uses, she will be nearby in case she overdoses. She is not sticking close to prevent her from using. She's there as a backup."

His words slice and dice, words I don't want to hear, despite recognizing his logic. Our eyes make contact, mine tired, longing for release. He reaches over the table to touch my hand. What else is there to say. I nod my head. My voice is held captive for a moment. If I speak it will break.

Evening. Darkness falls. Heather has gone out. Her smoking addiction calls to her as well. We do not allow smoking in the house, so she must go out into the night air. She walks, her face upturned to the stars in the blackened sky, brilliant and beautiful. She finds a spot, not sure where, but it is nearby. She stops, finding a quiet place to meditate, smoking, drinking her coffee, sweetened with lots of sugar and cream. She gazes up into the night sky. She loves these moments of solitude, of peace.

Meanwhile, Sarah awakened. She descended the stairs and quietly slipped away, out the door into the cold, dark, winter night, driving towards infinity, her next fix, her moment of euphoria. Soon, Heather walked in the door, trailing the strong smell of tobacco. She noted, "Sarah's car is gone. When did she leave?"

"Not too long ago, maybe ten or fifteen minutes, I told her.

She looked at me with accusation.

"Why didn't you stop her?" How do you stop a train wreck, a car with no brakes; a person with urges so strong she will do anything to fulfill them? A pregnant pause ensued between us as I looked at her. She gets it, knowing her question is unanswerable as she uttered, "I'm sorry."

She called her sister several times. Sarah finally answered. Her speech sounded slurred, almost unintelligible. Heather heard what sounded like the phone hitting the car floorboard. The connection died. Heather was frantic.

Her eyes wide with fear, she asked me, "Mom, can I have your car keys? It sounds like she dropped her phone."

I handed them to her mutely. We were wild with worry.

"Mom, where's the Narcan?"

I told her; she grabbed it, stuffing it in her purse.

"Can I borrow your cell phone?"

I gave it to her.

"I'll call you when I find her."

She rushed out the door without shutting it. The cold night air rushed in. It surrounded me, reinforcing my squeezing cold heart, heavy with an unbearable fear. Walking over to the door I closed it tightly, as the waiting began. Unease. Dread. Roger watched TV. I paced. I puttered. I could not focus. My mind raced. *Please, God. Please, God.* My supplications seemed so futile. An hour passed. An eternity. The phone finally rang. It was Heather. "I found her. She's okay."

Our sad, depressed Sarah. She is lost, so lost! And Heather, not knowing what to do. Soon, they walked through the door. They mingled for a moment in the living room, then Sarah headed upstairs. Heather followed her. We heard them talking, their voices muted. Secrets.

Heather came downstairs and asked, "Mom, can I borrow twenty dollars? Sarah wants to go out with a friend. Her friend is picking us up, so Sarah will not be driving. We're going to a club."

Warning bells, red flags. "No, I can't give you any money. I'm sorry."

A moment of disappointment flashed across her face, but she quickly hid it. She walked into the office, opened the file cabinet and pulled out the bottle of rum we had hidden. I had bought it a couple of weeks ago with the intent of making strawberry daiquiris. I made only one. It tasted too strong for me, probably since I rarely drink. With the intent of giving it to my son later, we tucked it away. The bottle was nearly empty. We had put it away almost full. Sarah must have found it and told Heather where it was. I knew I should have thrown it out. She poured several ounces into a glass and downed it. "I'm going to need this," she said.

Sarah came down the stairs and they headed out the door. It was nine p.m. I tried to stay awake, hoping they would be home before exhaustion forced me to go to sleep, but by eleven-thirty, my body rebelled. I needed to sleep. I slowly ascended the stairs to my room and climbed into bed. Closing my eyes, I drifted away.

The phone was ringing beside my bed. Groggily, I glanced at the clock. It was two a.m. My grogginess instantly disappeared as adrenaline surged. I answered. "Hello."

"Mom, we're stuck without a ride. Can you please come get us?" It is Sarah.

"Where are you?"

She told me. I woke up Roger to explain what was going on, and that I was heading out to get our daughters. He mumbled a response, turned his face away and went back to sleep. I was on my own.

Twenty minutes later, I had parked on the side of the street in an area long recognized *as the seedy part of town.* A huge Catholic church owned this corner, its steeple rose high overlooking the hill and its congregation. Its congregation varied, many are poor, yet it demands its dues as it overlooks the frailties and sins of those who congregate.

A cat, sleek and black slinked by and I saw dark shadows, forms, movement. My daughters? One tall and curvy and the other somewhat shorter and slender.

The lesser shadow reached down and scooped up the cat, holding it in her arms. Cradling it. Running her hand along its thin frame as she stroked its fur. This is Heather, her heart always full of kindness and compassion for those who seemed to be lost or in need. I knew if she could, she would have claimed the small, thin feline out wandering late at night. She cradled it in her arms for a moment, close to her chest, then lowered her face towards the cat, pressing her forehead against the cat's feline head. Bending her knees toward the frigid ground, she opened her arms letting the cat go. Its small feline form disappeared into the shadows.

Their breath rose white in the frigid air. They wore no coats. They carried no purses. They hugged themselves for warmth. Sarah quickly opened the passenger side door and climbed into the front seat. The car's heater was on high blowing its warmth around us. Heather climbed into the back seat behind me. Sarah glanced my way. "Thanks for coming to get us, mom. I'm sorry we had to wake you up and make you come out in the middle of the night."

She appeared to be crying, silently shaking as she held her head in her hands. Heather was silent. Secrets.

I asked, "What happened? Where are your coats and purses?" Silence. Are they trying to figure out how to respond? Of course, they are. Heather answered my questions.

"Sarah's friend had an emergency and had to leave. Her babysitter called her. Her daughter was sick. She left so quickly we weren't able to get our coats and purses."

"Where does she live? I'll go get them," I volunteer. My car keys were in Sarah's purse and that concerned me, as well as their missing items. They had come home and left so quickly earlier that evening that I had forgotten to ask for them.

"No, we'll take care of it tomorrow," Heather quickly told me, going on to explain, "She lives about twenty miles away. It is too late tonight anyway. Besides, her daughter is sick."

I glanced at Sarah. "Are you okay?"

Sarah was silent. Heather responded for her. "She has a headache, mom."

The twenty-minute drive home passed quickly. The streets empty. We only saw one car as we drove home. It was quiet, stillness encroached. The streetlights reflected a few snowflakes under their bowed domes of light. We passed by buildings darkened and shadowy, presenting an eerie presence. The short trip felt surreal, unearthly.

Finally, home, we entered our warm home—a haven from the dark, cold night we just left behind. No one sitting on the couch to greet us, to ask us how things went, if we were alright. Roger still slept in his room never making a sound as we came into the house, shut the door and locked it. My daughters headed upstairs quickly to Sarah's room and I escaped to mine. Exhaustion swept over me as the adrenaline eased away.

When I later shared with Sherry that night's escapade, she looked at me in disbelief.

"Why would you go out to get them at two a.m.? They are adults. You should have let them find their own way home. I would never do that to you."

"Sherry, you wouldn't have put yourself in such a position anyway."

"You're right, I wouldn't!"

"I couldn't not go and get them, Sherry. Not the way things stand."

Sherry shook her head.

Much later, the truth was revealed as to what really happened to their ride. Sarah's friend had abandoned them at the club to drive off somewhere with her boyfriend to do drugs. They were pulled over by the police, who found drugs in their possession. They were arrested. No sick daughter with a babysitter. More lies. More secrets.

~

SHATTERED

Heather had been hanging tight with her sister for almost a week. Her anguish and exhaustion showed in the tautness of her face, the hollow, helpless look in her blue eyes. We stood at the top of the stairs. She had come out of Sarah's room, catching me as I was about to enter the bathroom with the intention of cleaning it. Sarah had left, silently, a shadow, not saying a word.

We stood facing each other, inches away, but the distance between us felt like an ocean. So many issues remained unresolved. A sea of emotions and turmoil continued to exist between us. Heather revealed to me earlier her own feelings of loss. Her belief that she is considered as the black sheep of the family. She has long felt misunderstood, unloved. While it is true many of her choices have caused us grave concern, worry and yes, anger, she has always been loved. Always!

"Mom, I think I'm going to go home tomorrow. Sarah told me to go back home to take care of my family and to back off; that she did not need me all up in her business."

The look in Heather's eyes hurt my heart. She continued to talk, her words rushing out. "Sarah tried to soften her words though. She said I know you're worried about me. I appreciate that you want to be here for me, but I feel guilty you are here when you should be with your family. Your kids are missing you. You need to go home."

Her voice filled with anguish. "She needs me mom. I don't want to leave her alone. She is closing herself off. She won't let me in. She's my sister! What can I do?"

Conflicted, I dreaded her leaving because I felt Sarah may be safer with Heather nearby, but the tension was palpable, and I knew her family needed her. Sarah had branched off, heading down a dark road, uncharted, leading to a place I did not want to even think about. It was unfathomable.

Uncertain what to say, worried that whatever I said may come out wrong or be misconstrued, I weighed my words carefully. "I don't know what either of us can do at this point. We're in a tight spot. I know you love her. I love her too. But Sarah is stubborn." But the truth—truth we still unable to face? It was not that Sarah was stubborn—she was battling her addiction, and her addiction was winning.

The following morning at eleven a.m., I went upstairs to ask Heather when she wanted me to take her home. She and Sarah were sleeping soundly. I made the mistake of awakening them. Heather's kids once told me that they never wake up their mom from a sound sleep. Surprised and curious I wondered about this statement, so I asked, "Why?"

Their response?

"She gets mad."

Ever the person who tries not to press for information unless it is ready to be shared, I did not pursue this brief conversation. It was some time ago. I had forgotten all about it, but this morning, Heather's reaction brought it back into focus, clearly and irrefutably.

"Why are you waking me up? I was dreaming. I was in a good place. Why did you wake me up?"

Heather's voice grew louder, her agitation evident. She angrily threw the covers back and got out of bed. She turned to face me and what I saw startled me. Rage. Sarah burrowed deeper, covering her head, groaning a bit, not saying a word.

"I was finally sleeping soundly and was dreaming. It was a wonderful dream, and I haven't had a dream like that in a long time! I haven't been able to sleep well for days and you woke me up!"

I took a step back. "I'm sorry. You told me you were going home today. It's getting late and I wanted to check in with you."

The next few hours Heather expressed her anger and despair loudly, as I remained largely silent. Understanding swept over me. Was she struggling with the same thoughts as my own? Was her anger really an expression of fear and terrible realization? Had she realized her inability to stop Sarah's downward slide into oblivion?

She could not rail at Sarah because Sarah had escaped, silently and swiftly. While Heather gathered her belongings, Sarah had gotten up and showered. She took off, leaving her sister behind, not saying a word. Heather had brought tons of laundry, which she bagged up and dragged outside to be loaded into the van. It had taken her the entire week to do it all. Their washing machine was broken and had been for some time.

Heather intermittently cried, then vented, her eyes sunken and red. Emotionally spent, neither of us could voice our true fears. The truth of that moment? I was present, but Sarah was gone, so who else to vent her fear and anger towards other than me?

In the kitchen. Almost ready to leave. She paused beside the table to make eye contact. The final thrust, straight through my heart. "If she dies, I'll never forgive you. You are responsible for this. I'll never forgive you!"

Stricken and sick of heart, I was mute. I could not refute her words because in that moment, I did feel responsible. The events leading up to this day rested squarely on my shoulders. I failed to protect my daughters in so many ways.

The hour-long ride was agonizing. Roger's eyes stared resolutely ahead as he drove. The sound of Heather's sobs seared me. Tears streamed from my own eyes. We both, whether consciously or otherwise, knew what was coming, but were simply unable to articulate our fears. To voice our fear was impossibly painful. The inevitable was rushing toward us; we were helpless to prevent it.

As we drove her sobs gradually slowed and stopped. Emotionally exhausted, she had fallen asleep, allowing her a few moments of reprieve and peace. Her denial was shattered. I had no inkling that we would not speak or see each other again for nearly six months.

STOLEN MOMENTS

The question lingered, festering in my mind. What if Heather, instead of opposing us, had supported our efforts to urge Sarah to accept treatment, would Sarah still be with us? Before I understood the true nature of Sarah's disease, I thought those were all stolen moments, and my anger blazed against Heather.

However, I was forced to acknowledge another truth. Sarah's disease had progressed to the terminal phase. We would have lost her soon anyway. Sarah had long ago lost herself. The disease of addiction had robbed us of the Sarah we once knew and loved, consuming her, engulfing her in a world we would never understand.

An epiphany surfaced. Heather grabbed those moments, using them to reestablish a sisterly bond, something they both needed desperately. Yes, she stole them away from us in the sense of coalition as a family unit to urge Sarah into treatment. However, she did not realize, and could not accept the truth; Sarah's addiction was deeply entrenched. She believed if she reinforced and strengthened the sisterly bond, Sarah would recognize she was not alone. Her love would reinfuse Sarah with hopefulness and purpose—giving her added strength to overcome her inner demons. The reality though?

None of us during those moments understood the truth—the truth that Sarah was battling a devastating and deadly disease.

Heather made a conscious decision to leave her family distractions and responsibilities behind to focus on her sister, completely and unequivocally. I used those moments to reconnect with Heather. We used those moments to try to find ourselves as a family again. Stolen moments? Perhaps, but they were also a gift of reconnection, and finally, painfully, realization.

Two fear-filled, stressful weeks passed by in a blur after Heather left. December 16, a day that will forever be seared in our memory—my memory. Sarah had walked through the front door in her quiet, resolute way. It was mid-afternoon. I stood at the stove cooking dinner. The tantalizing aroma of baking haddock and roasting zucchini seasoned and drizzled with a touch of olive oil swirled in the air. I turned to greet my youngest daughter with a smile.

"Hi, Sarah!' She paused for just a moment.

"Hi, Mom, that sure smells good."

"Thanks! I am making you a plate. It will be ready soon."

She flashed me a wan smile but did not say anything else as she ascended the stairs to her room. I did not know she walked upstairs with a small packet of illicit drugs, opiates, dirty heroin contaminated with fentanyl hidden in her pocket with the intent to insert a needle, the syringe full of this poison into her arm. I did not hear her as she collapsed from her desk chair onto the floor as the drug quickly reached her heart causing it to stop beating. I just did not know that today would be the day...Sarah's last day…with us…on this earth. The day when I would find Sarah on the floor in her room not breathing, her fingertips blue, a syringe of poison in her half-opened palm.

~

REMEMBRANCE

WHO ARE YOU DAUGHTER OF MINE? PLEASE GIVE ME A SIGN. YOU DID, YOU GAVE ME MANY. I MISSED THEM.

Sarah, I miss you so much. How could I not know the extent of your inner turmoil? How could I not realize how dark your world had become?

The pathway to this moment has been long and winding. Reflection may bring clarity to the moment, but reality is stark and unrelenting. The signs were there. Missing them will forever haunt me.

If I could turn the clock back, how far would it go? I do not know. Would it go to the point when I knew that I was pregnant with Sarah? I did not plan her pregnancy, but there she was! My fourth and last child. My baby. The doctor had said, "No more babies." What do doctors know?

~

The moment I knew you were on the way, I loved you. You brought me so much joy even though you were unexpected. Oh, Sarah, you were loved so much. I will always love you. I will never stop loving you even though you are gone.

When you were ready to emerge from your nurturing cocoon of warmth to meet the world, you were in such a hurry!

~

The doctor checked on me and said, "Oh, it's going to be awhile yet."

I knew differently. My fourth child. I knew my body. I knew the signs and I told her, "No, when I go into transition it will happen quickly."

She shook her head negatively, disbelieving me, and left. The reason I chose a female physician to deliver my last child was with the hope I would be treated differently this time, with the instinctive knowledge that only another woman can offer, a woman who is also a mother. A woman who had experienced the miracle of birth and understood that a woman knows what she knows; is in tune with her body and the birth process, especially so when the birthing process is reoccurring.

It was not long after the doctor left before Sarah was ready to be born. The nurse checked our progress to observe the crown of her tiny head emerging from the birth canal. The cord was wrapped around her neck.

"Try to hold back. Don't push. Don't push," she urged.

She rushed away. Her voice echoing the hallway.

"I need a doctor. Now!"

The doctor who delivered Sarah? I laugh now with the irony of it. He was the one I had fired. I hired a female OBGYN and ended up with the same doctor who had delivered her sister and brother. I remember clearly his demand.

"Don't push. The cord is around her neck. I need to remove it."

I watched in the mirror with great interest as he unwrapped the umbilical cord, once, twice, then a third time. She was being strangled, and I had no idea.

"Okay, you can push now."

~

Only one push and you were born. I watched you take your first breath and listened as your newborn cries reverberated across the room. As you were placed in my arms, it was love at first sight! My baby girl, my last-born child. So beautiful! How was I to know you were only a loan? A precious gift!

A memory flashes in my mind. I am holding Sarah in my arms. Her father walks into the room, home from work. I am sitting in the bent-wood rocker, rocking her. She lifts her head off my shoulder to speak these words for the very first time.

"Hi da."

She smiled widely and lifted her arms up to him. Oblivious to this monumental childhood milestone, he walked right by. Her face quivered and her smile disappeared.

I stopped him.

"Did you hear her greet you?"

He looked at me blankly. I repeated Sarah's first words and actions to him, but his response was lukewarm at best. Were his inner thoughts that much of a distraction he could not observe this milestone his daughter directed toward him? Did he have to go to the bathroom? Was he hungry and eager to eat? I do not know. I do not remember — it was so long ago. I do remember Sarah's reaction to her dad's inattentiveness and apathy though.

If I could turn back time, I would stop him in mid-stride and put Sarah in his arms. I would tell him to hug her closely to his chest, to smile and play with her, to reassure her that he loved her. Nevertheless, I am powerless to rewind time. I am powerless to change the past. All I can do is move through time and live my life, and with each breath, Sarah lurks in the shadows of my mind.

~A lifetime of sadness for you daughter of mine. I am so sorry, but these are just words, aren't they? I remember a conversation we once had. We were

talking about the importance of apologizing, of saying, "I'm sorry." Your discernment set me back when you said, "Those are just words. If someone is sorry, they need to do more than just say the words."

I know you knew how much I loved you, but you could never love yourself. The hurtful words you repeatedly heard from your father as a child sunk in deeply, silently wounding your heart, affecting your self-worth to an extent I never imagined.

Sarah, you were beautiful! You struggled so hard with self-image, comparing yourself with your sister, Heather. Her body was angular, slender. Yours was softer, curvier. Different body shapes, similar facial structures. Two blonde-haired children. Her hair fine and straight, like mine. Yours voluminous with natural waves framing your face. Both of you beautiful in your own ways. Two little stars circling each other, as others watched, judged. Different, yet so similar. Because your souls were kind, watchful, curious, insightful, and sensitive.

A few days before you died, I remember you uttered these words. They echo in my mind, forever haunting me. You walked into the kitchen to greet me, wrapping your arms around me. My heart jumped joyfully as your tall frame bent over to hug my much shorter one, enveloping me in your warmth.

However, your words chilled me as you whispered in my ear, "I love you mom. I just wish I loved myself as much as you love me."

I felt your tears, wet against my cheek. My heart plummeted. I simply did not know what to say as my tears mingled with yours. We stood there in the kitchen for moments, a memory frozen in time, as we held each other.

My Sarah, my poor Sarah. I could not reverse the damage no matter how much I loved you. My love could never replace a love you longed for from a man who you saw as incapable of providing it—your dad. The result? You looked elsewhere, always met with hurt and disappointment.

Nine days before Christmas I found you, in your room, alone, your veins full of drugs that you injected to fill the void of your own inner sadness, drugs that stopped your heart, leaving mine broken beyond repair.

~

IF ONLY

If only I had stopped Sarah from going up to her room. If only I had stopped preparing dinner, walked over to her and hugged her tightly, urging her to sit down at the table as I finished preparing the food, would Sarah still be with us? Could I have stopped the inevitable?

But she would not eat a meal at the table when her dad was present. She would not subject herself to his onslaught of questions, causing her to feel as if she were being interrogated; to his often-demeaning comments, that always made her angry or worse—to cry. She would rather eat alone in her room, avoiding family meals altogether She would rather eat alone in her room or avoid family meals altogether. The damage had been done, irreversible.

I have been forced to realize that preventing Sarah's death was never in my power. She was in the grip of something so powerful I cannot even imagine its hold on her. Here I sit, wishing for the impossible, and knowing I must accept the reality that she is gone forever.

The days slowly, inexorably pass. I do not die. I continue to breathe and do the things one must do. I wander the rooms of this house, taking care of what is necessary. I cook, clean, do the laundry, but I am mostly silent. Conversation between Roger and I is stilted, strained. Inside I simmer with anger. I try to bury it beneath endless grief and sadness. Roger speaks of nonsensical things: the weather, the news, his physical pain. He will ask about plans for dinner. My responses are often monosyllables tinged with irritation, annoyance bordering on disgust, hate. He often glances my way and asks his never-ending question, "What's wrong with you?"

"Nothing," I respond.

Early on, I would attempt to explain my feelings. "I'm grieving. I am sad and angry. I'm processing Sarah's death and everything that led up to it."

He would just shake his head, in his usual manner saying, "I'm grieving too."

His words have little meaning, although I try to recognize his grief, but his grief does not match mine. I recognize he loved her in his own way. But Sarah never felt his love. His relationship with Sarah had been lost a long time ago. Did they ever have a true father/daughter bond? No, sadly they did not.

It is hard to hold in the anger day after day as it roils inside darkly, insidiously, unhealthfully. Love and Hate. Two powerful emotions. One positive, full of light; the other dark, hurtful. It takes a toll.

I eat because my body tells me to, then I eat because the emptiness in my heart needs to be filled. When my husband touches me, I flinch and pull away, although part of me longs for an embrace, to feel comfort, reassured that I am lovable. I am lonely, so lonely. The emptiness has left me feeling hollow, wanting. How can I love when I feel so much guilt and self-recrimination? How can I love a man who in these moments I loathe?

In the quiet moments, I hear Sarah's voice. She walks with me as I plod through this thing called life. Moments come when I smile or laugh, but seldom while here in this house. I pack up things to escape the sounds of Roger's voice for just a little while and the never-ending sounds of the TV. I stuff the essentials into a bag—laptop, Sarah's journals, iPhone, water bottle, and flee.

I walk the trails listening to the birds chirping and watch a squirrel scamper away. I hear rustling in the trees and feel the wind against my cold skin, as I reach up to remove a wisp of hair from my blue eyes. The clouds above me change from wispy white to grey and mauve and sometimes I watch the sun as it begins to set across the water. Sunsets of purple and yellow, pink and golds, swirls of color and always different.

I have captured birds in mid-flight with a click of my camera, their darkened, shadowy form and outstretched wings feathery and light. I find a place to write, a cafe, interstate rest stop, a restaurant, any place with Internet, until I can steel myself to return home, to a house with no warmth, no sounds of laughter, no music, no happy sounds.

As I park the van in the driveway, I sit behind the wheel to ready myself. I gaze at the horse chestnut tree we planted so long ago when we first built our home—just a seedling then. It is now thirty feet tall, a haven for birds and squirrels. It is beautiful in late spring, filled with white cone-like blossoms with pink stamens. In the fall, its spiked fruit ripened, falls to the ground, breaking open to reveal glistening dark brown chestnuts. Inside this nut is something lovely, ivory fruit —nature's bounty. The squirrels busily ferret them away, but with inner wisdom, they still leave behind many to feed deer and other critters.

I look at our closed house. When I leave Roger behind, I leave window blinds open to invite the sun, welcoming its warmth and light. Returning they are often closed as he sits on the couch facing the TV. Sometimes he naps—his mouth wide, snoring softly. I enter, glance his way but there are no smiles. Our eyes meet briefly then slide away. The house has become a house of mourning, chilled, cool.

My friends give me advice. "Give it time…It takes time. The time will come when your pain eases, smiling will become more natural, and you will find yourself laughing again. Give it time."

Time seems to creep when sleep is elusive. When it comes, dreams swirl around me and sometimes I awaken to tears that have coursed down my cheeks, unbidden in the dark of night. I dream of Sarah. She smiles at me and holds her arms out to hug me tightly. She talks to me, comforting me, reassuring me.

"I'm good, mom. Do not worry about me. I am happy. Do not cry mom. It was not your fault. I am sorry I hurt you. We will see each other again. Be happy mom. I love you."

When I awaken, I smile between the tears, because you have reached out beyond the veil to comfort me.

I once asked Roger if he ever dreams of Sarah. He looked at me blankly, "No, not really."

I wonder if he is telling the truth. For me these dreams are gifts of love. A love between a mother and daughter. Love is truly amazing. It is so strong that it can reach out even beyond death.

SHARED CONFIDENCES

SARAH WALKS BESIDE ME… HER JOURNALS CALL TO ME…

February 14, 2017

Somehow, I find the courage to pull out Sarah's journals and begin to read. I am in California, in my sister's home. She is nearby, just across the hall at her computer. She is a registered nurse by profession, but her passion is photography. Her subjects; flora and fauna, which she sees with an eye that transforms her images into art. It seems that the animals pose for her, as she captures their souls in the lens of her camera. She can capture a dewdrop on a rose, a deer pausing to glance her way with liquid brown eyes, an osprey in mid-flight, sunlight glistening off its outspread wings, a hummingbird as it hovers in her backyard. She photographs vistas portraying images of the sea, bluffs overlooking the ocean, bridges tall and graceful spanning empty spaces, building connections, a waterfall as it cascades over an outcropping of gray boulders. She inspires me. I must write. I will, soon…

It has taken me two weeks to muster the strength to search through my overstuffed suitcases, filled with clothes I probably will not wear in the warmer California weather. It is time. I choose Sarah's childhood journal first, the blue one. *Serenity Journal* is embossed on its cover. As I hold this journal in my hands, my thoughts remember a stranger's eyes filled with compassion. Someone I will probably never see again, yet who listened as my grief gushed out of me, unable to contain it.

Leaving Maine buried in several feet of snow, as the plane lifted off the tarmac into the strikingly ice blue winter sky I turned toward the window to see the starkness of winter gradually disappear. Counting my breaths, I knew Sarah flew with me. Her essence is forever a part of me.

Midway through the flight the man sitting beside me began a conversation. I have brought my own journal. It is open. A journal meant to inspire calmness, it's cover a monotone swirl of designs inviting the writer to add color. Opening the journal, I notice each page has similar designs waiting for the writer to personalize, identify, apply their brand. Lined pages waiting to be filled with script, with words-my words now. My thoughts, regrets, hopes, fears, desires. Once long ago, a child really, I dreamed of becoming an artist, one who would write and design children's books. I always loved color and its effect to lift one up and beyond their inner musings. I pulled out my gel pens to fill in the designs on the cover with vibrant pink, soft green, bright orange, deep purple

The middle-aged man sitting so close our elbows sometimes

touched, noticed my writing case filled with colored pencils and pens, and asked if he could borrow a pen. I lent him one, but he quickly touched my elbow. I looked at him askance. He handed it back. "It's out of ink."

"Oh, I'm sorry." I reached into the case and pulled out another. He thanked me and lowered his gaze, focusing on his own writing project as I returned to mine. The colors I chose were random, just something to do to distract me, to redirect my thoughts with the mundane choices of which colors to choose, rather than thinking about what I'm really doing; escaping, fleeing, running away, as far as I possibly can.

Finished with his writing, he returned my pen and began a conversation. He revealed that he was on a business trip, and then looked at me questioningly. "I'm flying to California to visit my sister."

I am not sure how the conversation turned, but somehow, we were talking about addiction. He admitted he had a long-standing history of abusing substances and was a recovering alcoholic. Without any prompting from me he revealed, "I was young and stupid."

What causes strangers to share confidences with one another? Is it the transient circumstances? The knowledge we will probably never see each other again? Is it just the need to fill in empty spaces? I did not want to talk. To share. I was too raw, too vulnerable. My emotions too close to the surface, but I did not wish to be rude. I smiled softly, made eye contact and attempted to engage. "What caused you to become sober?"

"I got married. My wife became pregnant and now we have a little boy. I need to set a good example for my son. My health was beginning to suffer too. It was time for me to make better choices."

The conversation turned again, and he began talking about the problems New England was facing with the influx of heroin. His hometown is Boston, Massachusetts. This conversation hits a nerve. Zing!

I take a breath, then another. I glanced at him, then away. Words seemed to surge out of me. I could not stop them. I did not want to talk about this, but he opened a portal and I cannot stop myself from stepping through it. “Maine had 376 deaths last year directly related to heroin use. Media and politicians say it is an epidemic. If that is the case, why is there so little treatment options? Finding timely and appropriate treatment is difficult, especially if one doesn’t have insurance.”

My emotions simmered just beneath the surface, my voice quivered. He asked me why I was so passionate about the subject. How do I escape from this conversation? Do I tell him the truth? My chest tightens. My throat constricts. I am in Sarah’s room all over again, seeing her stretched out form lying face down on the carpeted floor. Her fingertips blue. Her face deathly white. I blurted it out, regurgitating, spilling it because I could not hold it in. “My daughter recently died from an accidental overdose.” My voice broke. My eyes began to leak.

He glanced at me, then turned away to allow me a modicum of privacy in a place where privacy is virtually nonexistent. “I’m so sorry.” I didn’t mean to be inconsiderate.” He paused, then looked away.

Awkwardness and embarrassment between two strangers. Moments passed as he pretended to focus on something else, as I attempted to regain my own composure. I was seated in the middle seat. The woman to my left pretended not to hear our conversation, and my momentary expression of grief. She remained silent, averting her face as she glanced out the window. Nothing out there but space, empty whiteness. Better to glance away into nothingness than to acknowledge a stranger’s pain. A few moments passed before I was able to speak. Glancing his way, briefly making eye contact, I respond. “No, you were not inconsiderate. I apologize for losing my composure for a moment.”

“Don’t apologize. You certainly have a solid reason to be sad. Please accept my condolences. I truly am sorry.”

Kindness, warmth, connection. No glancing away. No avoiding someone’s grief. My appreciation swells. Despite the tears that glisten in my eyes I manage to smile my thanks. I whisper my appreciation for his words, “Thank you.”

I swallowed down the lump threatening to choke off my breath again. The conversation wandered away into small talk, meaningless, well-mannered, then just sort of petered away. We were descending now, getting ready to land. California. San Francisco and it was raining—hard.

~

CALIFORNIA

IT SEEMED EVEN CALIFORNIA SKIES WERE HEAVY WITH MY TEARS.

I arrived in California to a state washed away by torrential rains. Mudslides in the hills and flooding were daily news. A bridge collapsed near Big Sur. Hundreds of families cut off, relying on strangers to fly in supplies and to transport them to their livelihoods. I listened to the news commentator and watched the images of a bridge that had buckled from the excessive rainfall and observed the equipment that will demolish the only means of accessing the outside world for scores of families.

The media reported it would take at least a year to replace it. Will the new bridge be stronger with the ability to withstand changing weather patterns, intense winds and torrential downpours? California's drought is no more. Their dams are near bursting, their rivers overflowing. It seemed even California skies were heavy with my tears. The heavens so heavy they spilled and spilled.

A week passed before the rain finally ended. Sun crept out from behind the billowing clouds and the blue of the sky wiped away my tears. We walked the neighborhood past flowering shrubs, green lawns, pristine and well-kept, grapefruit trees dripping with ripened fruit. My sister picked a grapefruit as we walked past, round, firm, and red-tinged. The tree so laden with fruit its branches dipped low with their burden. Later I ate it; its tartness a treat to my taste buds, the freshest grapefruit I ever enjoyed.

Each morning, my sister, Brinna greeted me with a hug and coffee, dark and rich. We sat at her dining room table and talked. She was recovering from surgery, and my original purpose was to come and help her, to ease her transition, accepting her choice. We had formulated our plans months before. Long before Sarah died.

Brinna confided with me of her life-long gender struggles. She told me her plans to transition after all these years. Her children were now adults. Her marriage had long dissolved. It was time. I cried when she first told me. Our only sister had died from breast cancer. "I have a sister again!" I told her. Months of preparation ensued. Her transition from male to female finally becoming reality.

Brinna shared her thoughts with me one day when she stated, I know you came out here to help me, but I wonder who is really helping whom to recover and heal?"

My heart cracked open—again. My heartache so intense it physically hurt. I began to cry, and she held me. She knew what I needed. She simply listened and let me feel. I listened to her allowing her to voice her fears and concerns as she began her own next chapter in life. No judgments. We just loved and accepted each other.

A few days later in the midst of conversation, Brinna acknowledged something I had not yet shared with her. "She's here with you, isn't she?" I instantly knew what she meant but had been reticent of revealing.

"Yes, she is."

Our eyes met as she shared, "I felt her immediately when you first arrived." Grief, freshly awakened bubbled up and over. The fragility of my outward composure ripped away as the floodgates opened. She held me as I cried. As my tears subsided, our real sharing began. Now, I could tell her things I could not share with others, fearing they would question my sanity, perhaps because I was questioning it too.

Jehovah's Witnesses believe that when one dies they simply no longer exist. Their memory rests with God. They do not believe in a soul that leaves the physical body. They believe that the body is a soul. This faith teaches that demons pretend to be departed souls of loved ones. If one tries to communicate with the dead, they are communicating with demonic beings pretending to be a loved one, which angers God and damages one's relationship with him.

Jehovah's Witnesses believe they will see loved ones again in a resurrection after God destroys the wicked at Armageddon. They are taught that the earth will then be restored to a paradise, as God originally intended when he first created Adam and Eve. Before our original parents screwed things up by listening to Satan rather than to their creator, Jehovah God. Then, there will be a resurrection of all those who have died, bringing them back to life to live on a paradise earth. This will occur to fulfill bible prophesy such as stated in Revelation 21: 3, 4. "With that I heard a loud voice from the throne say: "Look! The tent of God is with humankind, he will reside with them, and they will be his people. God himself will be with them, and he will wipe out every tear from their eyes and death will be no more, neither will mourning nor outcry nor pain be anymore. The former things have passed away." (New World Translation.)

This scripture once gave me comfort and peace to my troubled thoughts, inducing hope of seeing my loved ones again in a new world where there was no pain or sickness. My sister, my mom, my dad, and many others whom I have loved and who have died. With Sarah's death, my belief system dissolved leaving in my heart so many questions and doubts. Adrift. Lost. It felt as if part of me had been torn away leaving an empty space that was impossible to fill. Is this what it is like to lose a child?

The explanation of sin and death is reiterated to all Jehovah's Witnesses. Who of us do not recall the ancient biblical story of Eve? Credited with causing human suffering and death? The original mother who allowed herself to be deceived; who listened to Satan rather than to God and ate from the tree of knowledge, then seduced Adam to do the same. God then expelled our original parents, Adam and Eve from the Garden of Eden. The first disfellowshipping. Humankind has paid forever for their disobedience. Their choice, as Jehovah's Witnesses interpret by scripture, resulted in sin and death... for all humankind until God decides to end this curse.

With Sarah's death, I came to question many of my beliefs. Since Sarah died, I have felt her presence with me continuously. We have been communicating inwardly ever since. I do not see her image. I know she no longer exists in the physical form, but her energy seems to swirl and gravitate near me. We converse, and her intent is clear. To encourage me, to lessen my grief and feelings of guilt. Some of her messages? "I'm happy now, mom. I am in a good place. It is so beautiful. I feel loved. Try not to be sad." The most important message she could give me? "Mom, it wasn't your fault! Stop blaming yourself. I made choices."

~

Oh, Sarah, you are my heart, and when you left, a piece of my heart went along with you. I miss and think of you every day. I feel you with me here in California. When I told you that I planned to go, you voiced your longing to come with me. Well, you did! I felt your spirit near.

You rode in the backseat as we drove around hairpin turns before reaching Redwood Forest National Park. You were there with me to gaze in wonder at the massive redwood trees that towered above us. I heard you whisper in my ear, "I'm here, Mom. This place is awesome."

You soared with the wind surfers in *Monterey while we captured their images. You stood by my side on the cliffs overlooking the Pacific as I snapped pictures. You walked beside me as I walked across Golden Gate Bridge in San Francisco with your brother, Donnie. Though I still shed tears of grief, the tears come less often. Your presence, your energy, comforts me.*

~

I opened one of Sarah's journals and turned the page to see her autograph. Her words have been waiting for me—calling to me. Sarah's older sister, Sherry, forever curious, read Sarah's journals right away soon after Sarah died.

She called me sobbing with grief and regret telling me, "I can't keep these journals mom." A week after taking them, she brought them back to me and I put them away in a drawer. Her admonition. "You probably shouldn't read them alone." When I left for California, the journals came with me. I could not leave them behind.

~

Your voice, your words greet me, Sarah. Your penmanship is sometimes rounded and neat, at other times scrawled and scrambled, spidery letters forming words, sentences, phrases and thoughts. Your objective for writing was clearly articulated. You hoped your words would be helpful to others. You expressed your hope that the future you, married with children of your own would perhaps dig them out to read.

Your words would cause you to recall your younger self, how you changed and evolved over the years. The words you wrote in your youth would stare back at the adult you, a contented, happy woman, perhaps with children. All you ever wanted was a happy family, something that others seemed to have, but somehow, our family could not achieve, at least not according to your expectations. Your goal of happiness and family was an elusive dream.

You struggled throughout your brief existence to articulate and share your thoughts. The person you longed the most to listen and understand you, your dad, was an angry, emotionally aloof, nebulous presence in your life, causing a deep void inside of you. You felt that your voice was never heard or respected by him or by others.

My lost daughter. Perhaps what I can do to best honor your memory is to share your thoughts. Perhaps I can amplify your voice with my own because you left behind something precious—your words.

~

MY CALIFORNIA JOURNAL

RECONNECTING WITH MY SISTER, BRINNA. FINDING MY COMPASS. LOOKING FOR MY TOUCHSTONE. CAN I FIND THEM?

February 14, 2017

I open my journal to write as I wait for the plane to depart. The Nor'easter is finally gone. My turn. Leaving for California. Cannot believe this is finally happening! I awakened at five a.m. My son arrived promptly at six a.m. to drive me to the airport in Portland. He helped me with my bags, depositing them at the baggage counter.

I have over-packed, unsure of what to bring. I know that winters in Maine are much different from winters in California, but since I have never been there, I do not know just how differently, do I? I am not even sure if I will return. Will my sister let me stay if I ask?

Donnie and I hugged our goodbyes. He is tall, solid. My son. I love him so much! But I must do this. I must go. We expressed our farewells.

"I love you, mom. Let me know when you arrive."

"I love you too! I will text you when I land in San Francisco."

I watched his long strides as he made his way out of the terminal, through the revolving glass doors. Signing, I turned away heading for security. Lifting my carry-on, I put it on the conveyor belt watching as it rumbled through the x-ray machine. Walking into the windowed scanning device, I stood still, allowing others to be assured, if they could see deeply into my heart, I was simply a grieving mom, not someone intending to harm others. But I am one of those who cause concern. Is it the stricken, vacant look? Eyes are windows reflecting one's soul. If they look closely can they see my pain? Or is it simply that I carry hardware imbedded beneath the outward covering of skin? Surgical scars are easily seen, but the scars from emotional trauma are much more difficult to see. They pass the wand inches from my body as I reveal to them the hardware that holds my body erect, undetected but by x-ray. Satisfied, I am allowed to move on. I found my gate. Breakfast. Hunger. Ordering a breakfast sandwich and a coffee, I found a place to sit. Not difficult in this small airport so early in the morning. I looked for a bathroom to take care of necessities, then walked back to the gate and parked myself.

My flight leaves at 10:30 a.m. It is 9:00 now. It is going to be a long day! Connecting flight is Newark, New Jersey, then a 1:00 embarking to San Francisco. Pinching myself. Yes, I am awake. Nope, not dreaming! Very quiet here at the airport, but I know that will change in New Jersey.

Hugged Roger goodbye briefly—his sadness was palpable. No smiles, or wishing me a safe journey, but that was expected. Did I say, "I love you?" Sadly, no. I am numb. I must get away. Sarah's death is still so fresh. Just two months ago—December 16. Still cry-especially at night.

Sarah and I spoke with each other last night. Crazy? No. Just processing. Not ready to let my daughter go yet. I do not think she has let us all go yet, either. Her presence, her energy lingers. She knows I need her still. The night before I was to leave, I heard Sarah's voice, expressing her excitement that I was actually leaving. A whisper in my ear, in my heart.

"So excited! You'll have fun, mom. I'll be with you all the way even if you can't see me, you'll know I'm with you."

"Yes, Sarah, I know you are my love." Just writing these words cause tears to form. But, strangely I am not crying at leaving home and Roger. A feeling of relief to leave that house—the house that has seen so much fragmentation, grief, and negative energy. I am searching for positive energy now. It does exist, right? It must, because I need it desperately.

Sunday Evening, February 19, 2017

Settling in here with Brinna. We are reconnecting as sisters rather than as brother and sister. She seems so much happier as she continues her journey of self-discovery a woman, something she only recently confided to me she has longed for since childhood.

I am proud of her strength as she embraces the gender she has always identified with, which is female. All of this blows me away. My intent in coming is to be supportive and help her heal from her procedure, but she is also helping me heal as well. Coming to terms with Sarah's death, but relinquishing self-blame continues to challenge me.

I feel your presence dear Sarah. You will always be a part of me. I am missing you-but somehow, despite everything that happens, life does indeed go on.

Yesterday, Brinna introduced me to a fresh fruit/vegetable market. The fruit here in California is wonderful. The oranges are so sweet and juicy.

I called your dad tonight just before he was going to bed. This three-hour difference in time can be tricky. He sounded sad and lonely. Oh well. He will be all right.

He has Boo-Boo for company, and Donnie, who has promised to check in with him now and then stopped in to visit him for a while today. I really need this time away. Enjoying the change of pace. Time to bond, reconnect, and heal. Goodnight dear Sarah. Be happy where you are.

February 23, 2017

The agenda for today? San Francisco and the Golden Gate Bridge! Wow! The skies are still gray, and showers persist, but it does not matter. I am here in California with my sister. The bridge is bright orange. As we pass over the bridge, I ask her a question. "Why do they call it the Golden Gate Bridge when it is actually bright orange?"

She laughed. "Do you really want to know? Do you want the short or the long explanation?"

"The short one will do."

She explained, "Well, what they really are referring to is the water. This area allows passage between the Pacific Ocean and the bay area. It provides easy access to trade; in essence, a golden gate of trade."

"Okay, that's cool, but really, I still think the bridge should be painted yellow or gold to live up to all the hype about it." We burst out in laughter. God, it feels good to laugh!

Sunday Feb 26, 2017

Heading to the coast today—the Pacific Ocean! The sun is finally shining! Still a little cool. I laugh to myself as I write this. It's February for God's sake. If I were in Maine, it would be frigid. Cool here is sixty degrees. Going to take pics! Last night—movies and popcorn on the couch. A little wine and lots of laughter and a few tears—not many though. I feel Sarah's presence always with me.

Thursday, March 2nd, 2017

Sunny and cool this morning. It is unusual for Brinna to be sleeping at this hour. She is always an early riser. I often hear her stirring at four or five a.m. Not me! She has appointments this morning, but yesterday she was more tired and drained and laid low for the day, which she needed to do. She overdid things Tuesday when she drove us to Moss Beach and photographed the sea otters. Did she make the effort to plan the day trip for my sake; to get me out of the house even though I assured her I was fine? Or perhaps she was tired of being inside too? We watched the waves from the Pacific roll in to touch and sweep across the sand. White clouds—banks of them hovered in the intense blue of the sky. We ate seafood at a nearby restaurant. The food was wonderful! Their white fish so fresh and tender it melted in our mouth. Scallops sweet and juicy.

March 3rd, Friday 2017

I dreamed of Sarah last night. Dreams are strange phenomena. She suddenly appeared and was beautiful! Smiling! I enveloped her in my arms and we clung to each other for a long time. Yet, too quickly our embrace ended. She felt wonderful—solid and warm. I told her, "I love you so much!"

"I love you too, Mom." She stepped back from me but held my hand and looked deeply into my eyes as she said, "You deserve to be happy. Stay in California or go back home; your choice but do what makes you happy."

"You look wonderful, Sarah. You look happy!"

"I am," she said smilingly, "Oh, by the way, I like Brinna. She makes you laugh. It's great to see you laughing again!"

I smiled at her. "It feels so good to laugh again. I am glad you like her. I will tell her." Sarah's eyes are pools of love. She squeezes my hand tightly and I hear her message in my heart. Looking longingly at her, I pose a question I already know the answer to. "It's time to let you go, isn't it?"

Her smile dissolved like the mist, as did mine. "Yes, it's time to let me go."

Our faces were wet with tears as we held each other. I was now conscious of my surroundings—lying in my sister's queen-sized bed. I could still feel Sarah's warmth and her presence, but she faded away as

I became more fully awake. Sarah was gone; my face was wet with tears, my arms wrapped tightly around my pillow.

March 6th, 2017

A time for healing, reflection, and moving forward. We saw a double rainbow yesterday, vibrant and colorful! Two rainbows, side-by-side. Two sisters side-by-side helping one another heal. We captured its translucent image as it quickly faded from view, swallowed by the clouds. A sign of hope? Could it be a reminder not to take for granted the beauty that surrounds us, perhaps? To not give in to our inner turmoil, sadness, guilt and despair?

Monday, March 14, 2017

Around two a.m. I emerged from a sound sleep to a sensation I had never experienced before. My entire body was, for a lack of a better description, vibrating—humming internally. I purposefully slowed my breathing, wondering if I was having some sort of heart event, but there was no pain, no true discomfort. A feeling of calmness surrounded and enveloped me in a warm cocoon of love and comfort. Was this a spiritual phenomenon? What was going on? Sensations of energy coursed through my body meant to recharge my weakened soul. That is the only way I can explain it. Since I live with chronic pain, this experience awed me.

I had awakened from a deep sleep and had been having an odd dream. I remember seeing a colorful Asian artifact appear in my dream and it was significant in some way. I approached it, reached out to touch it and at that moment I awoke to feel these strange, nameless sensations. I lay there for a few moments trying to gauge exactly what was happening to me. I was a living tuning fork, humming to a force, an energy, invisible, but still very much in touch with my own energy, my life force.

I have read that we consist of energy. We project some of that energy with each breath we take and then expel. Some who are particularly sensitive, can feel our energy, sense the type of person we are, feel our mood. Someone once told me that at death, the person's energy must go somewhere. Back to God? To the universe? To those that person loved?

Reaching for the down comforter that warmed me, I pushed it away, sat up and swung my legs over the side of the bed. Moonlight filtered through the slats of the blinds covering the windows creating an ethereal, cool, dim light into the otherwise darkened bedroom. Nature called, so I got painlessly out of bed, walked to the bathroom, then climbed back into bed to snuggle under the comforter. My body continued to respond to this invisible stimulus, this unknown energy force, until it slowly dispersed. Closing my eyes, allowing myself to live this moment, it slowly faded away like a rainbow in the mist as I eased back into a restful sleep.

Hazy sunshine awakened me once again to pain. My spine is slowly deteriorating as arthritic changes continue to emerge and make itself known, but I do not dwell on my pain. My focus is outward rather than inward. My mind relived the previous night's experience. Had it all been just a dream? No, it was a very real experience. It was new and uncharted, something that needed exploration.

Making my way out to the kitchen, the aroma of freshly brewed coffee welcomed me. Brinna was standing at the kitchen counter wrapped in her robe. She turned towards me with a smile and poured me a cup. Together we sat down at the dining room table to drink our coffee, our morning ritual. Dark and robust, it was truly a special moment each morning. A skill I have not yet mastered, and probably never will. My sister the barista!

Containing my experience was not possible; I needed to share, to talk about it. "Brinna, I had the most amazing experience last night," and haltingly shared, stumbling over my words, struggling to articulate, to explain what was nearly unexplainable. "What do you make of it? Am I certifiable? Have I completely lost it?"

She paused, gazed into my eyes for several seconds before

responding. "No, you have not lost it. Honestly, I am jealous! I think you experienced something very special. You are blessed to have such a spiritual experience. You have been through a lot. It is going to take time to heal, and it seems this may be a very real part of your healing process. I cannot explain it. I do not fully understand it myself, but I hope someday I will experience something like that. Wow! Just, wow! To think this happened in my own house!"

Many say the experience of pain lets us know we are alive. I beg to differ. Pain, whether physical or emotional distracts us. Pain demands attention causing its subject to lose focus on wonderful things; the beauty of life, of love, the sounds of nature, birdsong, a cool refreshing summer breeze, the beating of our heart as it thrusts our blood throughout the circulatory system, keeping us alive. Pain distracts us from breathing deeply, fully. It is a thief, a robber, designed to diminish enjoyment of life. Life is so short—too short for pain and its distraction. Why must we suffer with so much pain? It seems that Sarah's pain was simply too great for her to endure.

March 16, 2017

Busy day. We drove the twisting roads around hairpin turns up into the hills to see Redwood Forest National Park. We packed a lunch and sat at one of the picnic tables to eat our sandwiches and fruit as squirrels chattered. A raven watched us closely through his obsidian-like eyes. Was he hoping we would share? We walked the wooded trails and I lifted my face to gaze in awe at the gigantic trees surrounding us. God's handiwork. It astounded me, taking my breath. Pictures. I could not seem to take enough! As we drove away, I turned around for one last glimpse of the giants of the forests. Redwoods. Trees I had only previously seen in a movie or read about in a book.

We headed now towards the Pacific. Headlands. Towering cliffs overlooking the west coast. Both Brinna and I clearly felt Sarah's energy today. We knew she lingered near. Together, Sarah and I saw the Pacific Ocean for the first time.

I felt you, Sarah. You rode in the back seat and whispered in my ear, "Mom, this place is freaking amazing!" Okay, I must be honest, you did not use freaking, and as I write, I can hear your laughter. "Be honest, mom. Come on!"

SARAH'S VOICE

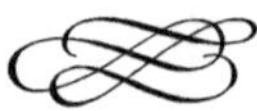

DETERMINED. ON A MISSION TO FINALLY GIVE MY DAUGHTER HER VOICE.

Sarah as a child

As I turn each page of her journal, I find her again, better understanding her. My heartache so intense I find it hard to breathe as my sobs swell in my chest. Somehow, I find the strength to continue reading even as my tears spill out of my eyes, run down my face and spill upon the opened page dampening it with my DNA, my footprint, my despair merging with Sarah's.

Perhaps as I share her words my journey of healing will continue.

Will others see a pattern of thoughts and behaviors to help them in their own meanderings as they journey through life? Sarah would have liked that. She hoped to become a writer; sadly, she didn't realize she had already achieved it. Thus, I will attempt to share her story. Our voices will speak to you, hers and mine.

Her journaling began in her thirteenth year, just a girl, tender and sensitive, as she struggled to form her thoughts, feelings and yearnings. Turning the pages of her initial journal as she first began to write, these words seemed to say it all.

September 5, 1999

"As I fill these pages with my thoughts and feelings I hope they will one day be of use and a source of encouragement (in some way) to someone else."

Sarah ~~

I flip back to the first page of her journal, when her decision to write about her world, her feelings, and who she thought she might be first began. Her words stare back at me and I see her ever-changing eyes; sometimes brown, sometimes green as they reflected her mood, but always wide, staring, haunting.

July 8, 1999

Dear Journal,

I think I have decided to keep a journal as most teens do. I want a record of my feelings and to remember how I used to think. Maybe if I get married and have kids this will be a useful key to understanding how they feel by referring to how I felt when I was their age. I think I best start by explaining who I think I am. I have been a Jehovah's Witness for thirteen years (only my whole life) and it affects every aspect of my life. Two years ago, my oldest sis, Sherry got disfellowshipped. So, I am not supposed to talk to her or acknowledge her presence in any way. If you have ever tried that, it is really hard. I think you will agree it is almost impossible.

Other things going on are mostly connected with my dad. I have so many problems with him and him likewise with me. He just seems always angry with me. Nothing I do is good enough. There is always something I have not done or have not done right. Every time I try to tell him something he has done that has hurt me, he just shuts me out of the conversation and will not listen to me. I feel no affection for him anymore. I only love him because he is my father. I do not think he is a good person or anything. That is enough for today. Bye, Sarah

Thursday, July 8, 1999

I think I should write at the end of the day. My dad just came home and immediately he tried to put the dog out. She ran toward me and as he grabbed her collar and gruffly pulled her out the door. I tried to stop him. He grabbed my arm and shoved me back into the chair. He even implied that I do not care about the dog. That is so untrue; she means more to me than almost anything. I would die rather than see her tortured.

Now he is yelling at my mother for everything. He thinks I do everything just to make him angry. He does not think I have reasons, and when I try to explain to him why he tells me to shut up. My sis, Heather, older by a year left to go swimming and left all the cleaning on mom and me.

I wish I could have a horse. Mom has taken me many times to look, but when things become more serious about buying, she sorts of chickens out. Sometimes I wish I could die. Everything is hopeless. I am almost never happy and when I am, my dad comes home. I try to spend time riding, but it is expensive; $25.00 for a trail ride.

When I get married, I will not marry a guy that looks or acts like my dad. That would be awful!! Heather is changing so much. I feel as if I do not even know her. She is so independent and does not care what my parents say. She only does what she wants. If she wants a stereo and mom says she has to earn it by good behavior, it is just – "fine, never mind."

July 11, 1999

Dear Journal,

I do not know what I am going to do. I have to choose whether I want to be a Jehovah's Witness. It is a hard decision. How can I give up what I have known my whole life? My dad is still being mean. I think in my journal I will call him "Roger." He was mad since I was not going to the meeting, so he slapped my head. Everything is the same, nothing changes.

I am not sure about therapy. I really don't want to go. I went Friday, but my dad had been a jerk and said mean stuff to me, and my mom didn't stand up for me. I went into therapy, but I heard my mom tell the receptionist I was being a brat and wouldn't get out of the van, so I thought fine, if she feels I'm a brat then I'll leave. So, I did. I walked to Kmart and Fashion Bug. I was going to go to the Kingdom Hall for a while when she came up the road by the rotary and pulled into the motel, so I got in.

I cannot talk to her anymore. I am sick of always being known as the mommy's girl and complaining to her. It's just that my mom has always been there, and she alone can stand up to my father and try to show him what he's doing is wrong. But he has to choose to open his eyes, to take his blinders off and admit it is his fault too.

July 11, 1999 1:16 PM

My sister, Sherry is coming pretty soon. We might do something fun. I'll tell you how it goes on the rest of this paper. See ya tonight!

Sherry came, and we went swimming and then had ice cream. Mom talked to Sherry for a while and then Sherry and I had a chance to talk on the way back from getting ice cream.

I wanted to spend the week with her. Mom would not let me, so I said I'm not going to any of the therapy sessions. I think I am going to Friday's session though. She said I had to be good and go to therapy.

I doubt I will go riding. No free adopt-a-horse horses. Somebody broke into (a local car dealership) and stole the cash register and it had no cash in it! Somebody is disappointed.

Bye!

~

For clarification, Sherry was currently disfellowshipped. I was still actively involved as a Jehovah's Witnesses and was experiencing deep inner conflict. How could I honor my faith when it seriously compromised my maternal love for my daughter?

I was walking a fine line and my balance was tenuously wavering. If I had allowed Sarah to leave to visit with Sherry that day, her father would have been angry. Facing his anger by making this type of decision he would have considered "wrong" was not a choice I was able to make yet. But it was coming...

~

Monday, July 12, 1999

Donnie is twenty-one-years-old! He does not buy beer because he does not like the taste. Mom told him that I know his "secret." I cannot believe she told him. He came in and started yelling at Heather, then me. Heather defended me...I cried. It would have been so much easier if he just told me what he did. I hate that I found unsuspectedly something I had not ever thought my brother would engage in. How am I supposed to feel? Heather feels it is no biggie – my parents? It is old news, but to me it is shocking, unbelievable and just scary. My bro... the perfect bro could have done something so stupid and something I never believed in a million years would ever happen. I will never get on his computer again. My bro with all his high morals engaged in premarital sex. Whoa!

Friday, July 16, 1999

Donnie had a discussion with me Tuesday about what I had discovered. I don't know what to think, and I hate finding out last! I know I should not have been on his computer and I am really sorry. I never knew or even thought he could do something like that.

July 18, 1999

Dad is being a real jerk. He spent half an hour just telling me what a horrible, ungrateful, disgusting little brat I am. I mean he has said it, but I still cry. I just want to die. I think my whole journal just reflects how miserable I am. I don't write every day. I don't know why. I have used the word "I" twenty-eight times on these two pages. How dumb. Maybe instead of just writing my feelings and emotions in this dairy I could do poems, stories, and songs also? I will try it soon. I don't feel as if Heather's friends, Patty and Pam are my real friends. I mean I know Dez is. I tell her almost everything. Except she doesn't know how much I'm hurting. I don't think I've ever really told her. I think that's something I need to resolve.

Lately I have been remembering the cute look **somebody** gets on his face when he is thinking about what I have said. I've noticed some guys do that and they are the ones I think are pretty hot. I think I have to learn I'm not ready for a beau. Every time I see one guy I think is cute and we're sort of introduced, then I'm going to think of him as a friend and I'm not going to make any moves unless he makes the first one. I think if I do that they won't feel intimidated. A lot of guys my age are more immature than me. That sucks! Bye, Sarah

July 23, 1999

I went to therapy today. I'm not sure if I would call it extremely helpful, more along the lines of somewhat helpful I suppose. Heather found two kittens in a box on the side of the road; a gray one we named Abby and a black and white one we named Maggy. I'm not sure how I feel. I think I'm definitely going back to school. For two reasons. I want to learn (feel I learn better there). And I want free band lessons. I don't want to homeschool because I know it would be extremely hard on my mother and she has enough stress without me adding to it.

I am still not sure if I am going to be a JW (Jehovah's Witness) or not. I probably will be. We are starting family therapy August 7 or 9 or something. Heather is missing again. We went to the beach today and the van broke down! Ugh! Just our luck. Maybe I should not take life so seriously. My dad says I am selfish and that I should think of other people besides myself all the time. Maybe he is right. But I do need to think about myself a lot right now. About what I want…what I need…stuff like that.

July 25, 1999

I am definitely going back to school. I should be going or at the meeting (Kingdom Hall) now but I am too depressed and worried about Heather. She left late last night because my mom took the kittens to the animal shelter. I still hate my mom for it. My father says I intentionally try to ruin and disrupt the family. That is so not true. I love my family. But right now, Roger blames me for everything and Heather for nothing. I always am the one to get ragged out by Roger. Donnie says I am overreacting and thinks I should talk to him. I avoid all confrontations if I can. I'm sick of crying all the time. I'm sick of being sad, unhappy and depressed all the time. But what can I do?

July 30, 1999

Nothing's different. I'm still crying every time Roger comes home. Why does he insist on belittling me every chance he gets!

I was reading Lurline McDaniel's book "When Happily Ever After Ends" and this 15-year-old girl's father kills himself. They went through so much pain because of him. Now I'm beginning to remember why I had those awful feelings of wanting to be dead. Now I'm experiencing them again.

He says I purposely try to ruin the family's happiness because I can't stand to see it happy. That is so untrue. How could he say that? I haven't done anything that bad have I? I can't stand this anymore. Please God let me die. Let me DIE!!! Be merciful and let be fall fast asleep and never wake up again. Don't make me face the cruel world and the pain of my father's words which he speaks so often. Why should I live when I'm considered to ruin the family?

The biggest reason I stay alive is to see that my dog, Foxy lady is properly cared for. I would hate to see her unhappy or not cared for or at the shelter. Why can't God be merciful towards me and let me DIE! I'm crying right now. Please God let me die.

August 1999

I wish someone would just listen to me and see how bad I always feel inside. It's like this heavy pain on my chest that goes away sometimes but always returns. I wish I could tell someone, someone who could help. I don't want to hurt anyone, just get rid of the hurt I myself have. It seems like it will never go away unless I die. If I knew where the gun was a few weeks ago I probably would be dead write now. I wish I was. Nobody understands that I need to feel as if I can get better, feel better. It seems as if Donnie is so concerned about his looks, his friends, and his social life he's too busy to hear me. How can I talk to him when he's always on his computer or gone?

August 25. 1999

Dear Journal, I really don't feel like writing, so I'll be brief. I am going back to school. Missy, Miranda, Melinda, and Kelsey are all in my class. I have a feeling if we do partners, I'm going to be the odd one out. My best friend, Jen is in is in my homeroom. Fighting continues.

Gotta Jet! Bye

September 5, 1999

Dear Journal, I've realized writing in you has become more of a chore, so I guess I've tapered off. I read the book, "Go Ask Alice." Alice is from a good family when she accidentally drinks a bottle of coke with the drug LSD in it. Then she keeps doing drugs. In it…her diary, she writes almost every day. And, if she doesn't she says, sorry I've been neglecting you. Roger was a jerk today. He shoved me into the wall. He told me:

1. That I did everything possible to make things miserable.
2. That I wasn't worthy enough to help him or my mother.
3. That I'm a selfish pig who thinks only of herself.

It's so depressing. I'm watching my friend, Dez's guinea pig, Felicity. She's cute. Dez went to New York to visit relatives. Heather left to see her friend. School started. I have a lot of homework and Roger is yelling at mom, saying she's an idiot basically. See ya. P.S. Things never change.

September 6, 1999

Do I have a sign on me saying, "Treat me like shit? Snide comments come flying out of my father's mouth aiming to hurt and injure…well, all I can say is, mission accomplished. You got me feeling like shit. I wish I was sleeping. Then I could escape. Escape from all these feelings.

I don't know what to write. Jen came over and we worked on a project. Roger is such a jerk! I can't do anything (neither can my mother). It's awful. I hate my life, myself and everything else. Please God let me die. Why should I be treated like this? Oh well, I guess it's not that bad. Mom and Roger are discussing how awful kids are, especially Heather.

To Roger I'm just the dumb fat one. I think I'll go work out. I feel… useless, hurt, upset and I want to cry like hell. I've cried too many times. Why can't life be good? It seems…oh never mind. Life sucks. That's all.

Roger is such a pig. He eats everything in sight. If there was no food he'd probably kill me for food. "Oh, sorry Sarah. I'm just so hungry. You don't mind, do you?"

Bye!

December 6, 1999

God, I haven't written in you for a long time. School has long ago started and I'm working at the Equestrian Center as of November. I can't believe I've lived so long without riding. It makes me so happy to ride. I love it!

Everything is the same. I started going to a counselor. I told her of several incidents which happened between my father and me. She reported them to DHHS, but so far nothing has happened. The abuse continues. He hurts me so bad when he tells me that I must be trying to break everything in the house slowly. It hurts my feelings.

I cannot believe how well writing in this journal helped me get my feelings out. Writing in a journal is purposeless unless you're trying to get feelings or emotions out. In my case, feelings between me and my father that is so hurtful and complex they must seem simple to other people.

Mom went to see the elders today to tell them what has been happening in our family. I wonder what they said. I know if I went I would have cried. I don't want them to see me cry.

December 7, 1999

I stayed home from school today. I'm not sure if it's more because I'm sick or more because I don't want to face the pressures of school. Anyways, at least my mom is supporting me as to what father is doing. Sometimes I feel as if dying is the answer, then I scold myself for thinking that foolish thought. Dying won't solve anything. It will only just get me out of the picture entirely as well as cause more unneeded hurt and grief.

I really don't mean to put my family through so much. But sometimes I think what am I really putting them through? And what are these strange marks I'm making on the paper? They are but letters that make up words that make up sentences. Sometimes I wonder, will this really help? Maybe. As I look back through the pages in my journal, I see how I express myself so well using these strange marks. It's early this morning and nothing has happened yet today. Well, I'm really sleepy. Goodbye.

Luv, Me

10:24 pm, December 20, 1999

If only we could stop our fits of anger and jealousy before we regret our actions. My sister just ruined a green frog candle that my friend got me for a New Year's gift. I'm using it to see to write now. Sarah scratched her fingernails down it and I'm rather pissed at her. I'm surprised she hasn't apologized. If she had I would simply have told her to go to hell.

Mom thinks I'm depressed. She wants to put me on meds for it. I said no way! I'm not going back to counseling. It's stupid. I don't want to have a relationship with my father and that's it. Why don't they just accept that????

Every weekend I work at a stable. I clean stalls, water buckets, and sweep floors. I throw down hay, feed horses and turn out horses. I groom horses and ride them. I love doing it and it has become a very important and crucial part to my survival and keeping myself busy, so I don't become depressed. I guess it's become my escape. Donnie hurt his tailbone snowboarding.

Gotta Jet. See ya!

Luv me

~

SEBASTIAN

THE REST OF MY BITCHING BOOK IS DEDICATED TO THE BEST HORSE IN THE WORLD – SEBASTIAN!

July 6, 2000

Hey sup?

I haven't written in here for like so long. So much has changed. Let's start with family. Donnie is disfellowshipped. Heather moved out and is living with her bastard boyfriend. I'm still working at the Equestrian Center. I practically *own* a horse there except I don't pay a dime for his keep. All I do is ride and take care of him. I am no longer always depressed and thinking about suicide. Life just seems so much more purposeful and happier. I feel like I've found something that I really love. It's great. I've made a new best friend. Her name is Heidi. She's twelve and kind of immature but she's really fun to hang with. I ride so much now...almost every day. I've ridden bareback, jumped, done dressage and western pleasure. I'm learning so much. It's such an experience. I love it. I think horses are going to be my career. I haven't been in a show-yet. But hey, life has still been great. Well, I got stuff to do so I'll write ya later.

Luv me lots, Sarah

August 30, 2000

Hey sup??

I'm still working at the barn. Heidi quit cause she's lazy. I still love my baby boy Sebastian. He is a Belgian Thoroughbred Cross. He does everything and is awesome except for his age, and the fact he isn't totally in shape. YET. OMG. Today was my first day of HIGH SCHOOL! It was actually orientation day but oh, well. It is so different from middle school. We have "agendas." We have to have passes every day and assignments. Jen is like, so obsessed with guys and sex it isn't funny. But that's cool. Christina's birthday party is next Friday. OMG!!! Heather and Sherry are pregnant! Heather is still living with her boyfriend, shit head. So, it is like so physical! I met this girl at the barn named Mia. She is the coolest. She's like, twelve though but oh, well! She's cool and acts so much older. Well, I gotta go. School is tomorrow. Ahhhhh! Luv ya.

Bye. Sarah

November 11, 2000

Today, my friend Holly brought her horse to the center and when the chores were finished myself, H and two more girls rode in the field. Sebastian did really well, although he coughed a bit. I jumped him out in the field. I did a cross-rail and a log jump. Sebastian seemed to love it.

(I skipped writing a few days [note gaps between dates] but I still rode!)

Monday, December 4

"Mary's Lesson"

Sebastian was awesome tonight! I was worried at first because he didn't eat his hay. (he ate his grain) We worked on doing simple lead changes. I ended up having a private lesson because Kay is lame. Because of that, me and Sebastian jumped. He was really good! We did a cross rail, vertical, and small spread. He seemed to have lots of energy and was so good. Mary said to trot poles with him (4) to strengthen his joints/muscles. She also said to practice the simple lead change, so he knows when he gets to the opposite wall going the opposite way. He needs to change leads. I'm so proud of him. The thrush in his hoof is getting better. Mary says to stuff a cotton ball soaked with iodine in the hole in his frog. So, I will take all her useful advice and use it!

Friday, December 15

Sebastian was tired and stumbled over the poles. Took him over a cross rail and he refused twice. Let "H" bee-bop on him bareback. (Didn't ride Saturday)

Monday, December 18

Sebastian was coughing a lot in today's lesson. We did counter canter and simple change to the other counter canter. We also did turns on the haunches which we had problems with because it's the first time I've done it riding Sebastian. I also did crossovers which Sebastian tried to refuse to do. I had my spurs on however, so it was easier for me to make him.

He wasn't listening to my leg a whole lot and in his rollbacks, he kept going to the inside with his butt. When I tried to make him, he kept doing it so "M" gave me a whip and I smacked him three good ones and he bucked and then listened to my leg.

Tuesday, December 19

I had a lesson tonight because I worked on Sunday and Saturday. Sebastian tried really hard, but we had to stop often because he was breathing really hard and coughing. We practiced counter-canter, simple changes, turn on the haunches, and jumping. He did serpentine jumps for the first time. This is hard! I've never done it before. I'm over the first one! My approaches were too short so that is something I'm going to practice.

Tuesday Jan 16, 2001

Mary didn't come today so Mom took me to the barn and I just rode for forty-five minutes. Mom watched for a while. She said I looked more "polished, comfortable, and overall better." I'm glad I look better. At the beginning, Sebastian's transitions were really great! They were just awesome. I think he must have gotten tired or something. I practiced changing leads over the pole. His coughing was six to seven on the scale. Worse than yesterday though.

Wednesday January 24, 2001

Amanda came up today! She invited me over to her house this weekend! I think I'm going to go. Sebastian was pretty good today. He didn't cough the whole time. Listened well to my legs. I rode him bareback and he was really good He wasn't convinced that I was okay when we cantered so he was hesitant. Maybe he was being lazy. I don't know. I can't wait to talk to the animal communicator Monday! "J" and mom are going to have an argument. I hope "J" wins so I can still go to the barn on the days I like going and so I can still work there. I don't think I could bear not riding Sebastian anymore. I would kill mom! (not literally) I would hate her though!

Saturday Feb 4, 2001

I fell off him for the first time! Kate and I decided to play a game-jousting with crops. Sebastian was really good. He coughed a bit during warmup but while Kate was chasing us he didn't cough once for 10-15 min. When we were galloping around the arena after Kate tagged me I was going after her but had Sebastian halt (trying to) but Kate got me laughing really hard and I fell off him as he tripped a little bit. I landed on my side and got the wind knocked out of me, but I got back on and cooled him out because he was really steamy.

Wednesday, Feb 7, 2001

Sebastian was really good. He listened really well and didn't cough once! I thought I better end early on a good note, so I rode 30-45 min. I may be going to Amy's this weekend or I might not. My mother is being a bitch and said because I didn't do the dishes I wasn't going to Amanda's. I'm so pissed. I don't think she'll go through with it but if she does she's going to go through holy hell with me!

Wednesday, March 12, 2001

I didn't ride Saturday because I missed work because Heather had her baby. Sebastian was pretty good. I was using "M's" big spurs so he was paying attention. We jumped over a little one with no reins on mane. I really need to work on it. It will help my balance.

Saturday, March 31, 2001

I am so excited because I am going to do a show in September with Sebastian! I already talked to mom about it and we are planning out when to buy the stuff I'm going to need! So, I really have to work hard on my position and looking good. I have to get Sebastian to stop quicker...Well, I have my work cut out for me!

Bye!

Sarah participated in the dressage competition and she was awesome.

I was so proud of her! We did buy all the stuff; new boots, riding pants, a black form-fitting jacket, a new helmet. Her excitement and nervousness were palpable that day. I watched on the sidelines, not fully understanding all that was taking place, but realizing how important this event was for Sarah. I wish I could have found the pictures I took, but my memories of that day will not be forgotten.

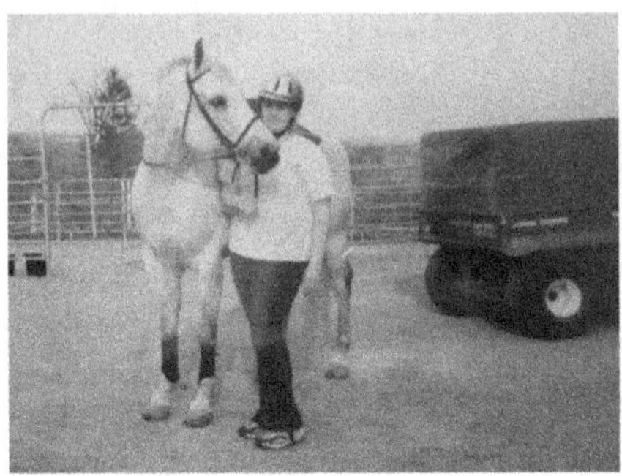

Sarah - Equestrian Center

FAMILY, CHANGE & BABIES

A year passed before Sarah began to write again. Sherry, Heather and her sister-in-law, *Ivy* were all pregnant with boys! Sherry gave birth first, to her baby boy, Sean February 2001. Heather's baby, Garry arrived in March. Donnie's baby boy was born in May. Sarah became an aunt and I became a grandmother plus three!

I was caring for Garry so much that he began calling me momma. At sixteen, Heather was just too young, a child herself really, to wrap her mind around her newfound responsibilities of motherhood. It was going to take time. She wanted to have fun—normal yearnings for someone her age. Her boyfriend was abusive, controlling and deeply into partying and drugs. When things got too intense, she would ask me to watch Garry. My attachment and love grew stronger every day and I felt more like Garry's mom than his grandmother. I struggled with the decision to assume guardianship of Garry.

Heather asked me several years later why I did not just take him. I knew from her father's experience as a child that the repercussions of such a decision could last a lifetime. Her question demanded careful thought because at the time what I did was instinctive. It did not feel right to take Garry away from her. I knew she loved him. A child needs their mother. I knew, not only from my own experience as a mom, but also from my observations of how her father was affected by his mother's decision to give custody of him to her mother (Roger's grandmother.) So, I attempted to explain to her why I chose not to push for custody of her son.

"I chose not to take him from you, Heather because I felt it was important for you take responsibility for Garry. A child needs his mother. I believe the decision made by your dad's mom to allow her own mother to raise him, Roger's grandmother, left deep emotional scars, forever damaging him. I also believe her decision left him feeling abandoned, unloved. He also carries with him the fact that his birth father refused to acknowledge him."

So much pain! I did not want to be the cause of more unnecessary pain, so I chose to be supportive, while allowing Heather to grow into her role as a mother.

Three new grandchildren in quick succession. We were all busy with these new additions to our family. During this time Sarah became more deeply involved with the equestrian center, making new friends and caring for Sebastian. She was blossoming. However, changes were coming soon that would affect Sarah deeply. Sarah began journaling again.

SARAH'S JOURNALING CONTINUES

March 26, 2002

Janet can't afford to keep Sebastian, so she wants to give him to me. He has heaves and is pretty bad off. I don't think he can handle the work that I want to do this summer because he is older. Also, "J" says if Sebastian stays Ryan goes so she can keep labor costs down. I think she just wants to get rid of stuff that is costing her a lot of money. I would love to take Sebastian and leave. I wish I could magically make him younger or something. I don't know. She always puts me in the hardest positions! If Kate takes him that would be just fine...If she can't I will but I know that will mean a lot of sacrifices on my part, but I think I'm willing to make them for Sebastian. He deserves to have a good home and I'm going to make sure he gets one and keeps it! I just know I can't let anything bad happen to Sebastian. He has been the love of my life and I know a certain part of me will always be totally in love with him.

July 22, 2002

I just got back yesterday from visiting Donnie. He and *Ivy* had a baby boy, Tim. I babysat him while they worked, and I totally had a blast with him. Donnie took me to NYC and on the subway! We also went to the Manhattan Mall. I got my name painted by hand with cool designs by an Asian man in CHINATOWN. Donnie is totally obsessed with Chinatown! We also went to the Rainforest Cafe where it's like a jungle atmosphere. It was in another mall in N.Y.

I'm listening to Dave, Donnie's Band-Space Between, an acoustic version and am reminded of Ryan for some strange reason. I kind of have a crush on him still! Not that I want to go after him like before, but I know I'm still going to blush when he's around and stuff, but I don't think of him hardly at all anymore.

I had a conversation with TR online and I think I have a crush on him now-not a serious one but he's really hot and funny-cool to talk to and probably a lot of fun to hang out with and be friends with. I know I'd love to be friends with him, but I don't know if little sis' are allowed to be friends with older bro's friends. Uh wahacare!

Okay, to change gears - Sebastian is being leased by Kate at her farm. He has a lot of lameness issues at this barn, so I'm concerned about his welfare. He is a little thin and is losing the muscle I worked so hard to get on him! I'm disappointed in his condition but he's still being taken relatively good care of. I haven't ridden him for so long and I miss him terribly. I still cry when I think about him and having to leave. I still love that horse with all my heart and I miss him so much! I always will be, and I know I will never have the same relationship with any other horse.

I don't think I'll be working at the barn this summer. I have my permit and will soon have my license. That means car payments, insurance, gas, upkeep and a ton of other new bills, including my cell phone. I definitely don't want to totally give up working at the barn because I really do love it. I just need to make enough money to pay my bills, so whatever it takes. TTYC!

P.S. I never knew how cool *Ivy* was until this past week. I will definitely be back!

~

IT'S COMPLICATED

Three years passed before Sarah began writing in her journals again. It is 2005. At age nineteen, she is delving into the complicated world of relationships and has moved out of our home. She quit school at seventeen, just one semester from graduating, but not without a fight from me. I did not understand why she was doing this. It made no sense to me. "Sarah, why? I don't understand. You are doing so well in school. You are so close to graduating!"

"Mom, you don't understand. School is so stressful. They force-feed you stuff that isn't even real. Useless. It does not pertain to the real world."

Despite my attempt to reason with her, she was adamant in her decision. Nothing I said could sway her.

"I'll get my GED, mom. Don't sweat it. I'll be fine." It doesn't matter whether I have a diploma or a GED. They both get you to the same place."

At eighteen she moved in with her boyfriend and his mother. He was abusive too. It seems that history repeats itself. Gradually, her goals shifted. She wanted to attend college, so she began working on her GED. She and Heather made a pact. They would work on their GED together and it became a competition to see who would achieve it first.

Forever struggling with the emotional void within, her love life was chaotic. Although Sarah and I saw each other often that summer, rather than sharing with me how deeply heartbroken she was; she articulated her sadness in her usual way – writing and journaling.

Her writing was expressive and deeply moving as she voiced her reflections, fears, sadness, regrets, and grief. It saddens me so much that she felt unable to share with me her fear-based thoughts. She was aware that I was struggling with my own challenges. Did Sarah want to spare me additional pain—her own? If only she had, I would have done my best to listen, comfort and reassure her.

She was aware I did not always approve of her choices. Undoubtedly, I would have thrown in my own counsel and thoughts, which would have been difficult for Sarah to hear. Her own internal voice, constantly second guessing her choices was hard enough to listen to as it was.

~

I WILL BREAK FREE

April 27, 2005

So, Bruno tells me that a lot of the time he'll watch me, and I just look lost. I guess I look exactly how I feel. I feel as if I've lost myself again. Like I'm in this huge swirling confusing tornado and I don't know how to make the wind stop blowing so hard. I feel so empty all the time. As if I'm nothing. I want to be in love.

The only times I feel true happiness is after a rewarding ride on Luna. She's such a gorgeous mare, and it's awesome to be riding once again. I'm so sick of men. But really, it's not just guys, it's girls too. I just hate everybody equally I suppose.

Wayne wants me to be his. He wants the same things I want except I don't want them from him. I can't talk to him. Every time we fight I just become silent because I don't feel comfortable talking and that frustrates him like crazy. He threw a movie at me tonight. Got really mad at me giving him "attitude" all day and just snapped it seems.

Oh well, I need to get my GED, a better job and my own place. I've had enough bullshit and I'm so sick of being treated like shit by guys. I honestly don't think Wayne is any different. I think he's just being nice to try to get me to fall for him. And once I do these little anger spurts that happen here and there are going to happen all the time. The first time he raises a hand, fist, or any object to hurt me it will be the last day that he will ever see or speak to me.

I need to fill this void I feel. It's eating me inside. I feel as if I'm slowly dying and it's horrible.

Till next time, Love Always, Sarah

P.S. What ken ya do?

September 10, 2005

Is this long wait worth it? Will you really change? Are you really trying or is this just another trick; a sick twisted turn that will only end up turning me in the wrong direction? Is marriage really what I even want? If our love was so true and meant to be shouldn't I know the answers? I know less today than I knew yesterday, and I just keep getting more and more confused. Everything I thought I knew is making me think twice. I'm going crazy and my heart is turning into ice.

Each time something fucked up happens it's like my life gets restarted. I'm back at square one; clueless, lost. Any direction is better than none, but none is all the ambition I can muster up.

I'm going back to the only thing I know; the only thing that never lets me down; that always touches my heart and soul; the consistent beat and movement it's encrypted in everything deep inside when everything else falls apart it's the solid foundation that never crashes in. It never breaks or lets me down. This special thing keeps me driven and enables me to keep it together. It's the love that burns so strong the passion I always succumb to-those damn horses! Without them I don't know where I'd be today-probably wherever we go when we pass. I've come so close to just ending it and so happy I chose not to because as bad as it gets I'd never want to miss out on LIFE!

What joys today will bring. I would miss all those things I used to say I didn't like because I really loved them, and if you could see inside my brain things would be so completely different. If only I could know what you really thought; what you've really wanted. I know what I want for myself, but I'm lacking the motivation to fulfill my dreams. Everything seems too hard and out of reach. I waste away each day closer to my last and without even realizing I just waste them all away.

I keep thinking I am going to open the door and see a reality completely different from my own and discover what I thought was real, never really was. I often wonder if I'm just another psycho who is living through their crazy life. I wish things were different. I can't do this anymore.

I wrote the same thing over and over-tried to change a part of it and couldn't. Couldn't bear to see it change.

Is it really wrong? Yes! Everyone has confirmed it for me; the fuck-ups will always continue. Those feelings—they aren't real; insecurities. Take some drugs and get your life together, then you'll be all set. For what though? What's next in this progression. My tummy tells me I need to eat. The mirror notifies me it's lying. I've eaten far too much, but I haven't drunk too much. Where's that damn bottle?

September 2005

Of all the things, I'd love to say to you. I hate you! Sometimes you'd do those stupid things and by the end of it you'd have me smiling, always eating right out of your hand. You fed me a lot over time-a lot of lies. But, mostly truths. Truths about life, about you...about me. You made me see things previously unknown to my deeply virgin eyes and heart.

I'm far from innocent anymore though. And as hard as I try sometimes, I can never move back, only forward-onward in this march through time. And is it time spent, so-called wisely, that matters most in one's sinful lives or is it the silly moments-those moments we treasure our whole lives?

There's only one thing I've always wished for. To know the happiness everyone else seems to already know. To create a family that cherishes each other, instead of one that hates one another, and why? Why did we put up with this; years of mistreatment, ill-spoken words spoken too frequently? Malicious attacks for what? After all these years, it's taken us away from each other. Far, far apart.

I feel closer to strangers than to the man who donated sperm to create me. Oh, a father is he-I beg to differ! Shouldn't a father care for his children; want what's best for them? He would never tear them down, especially not just to say he can. He stands up for them. Won't let anyone hurt them. He especially wouldn't do it himself. Above all though, he loves them more than he loves himself. A father, I have never truly known.

Sarah was voicing her deep feelings of hurt and acute disappointment in her father, feeling he had failed in his paternal role, crushing her, leaving her feeling bereft and unloved. I am not a psychologist, but as her mom, I believe the inability of her father to bond with Sarah affected her adult relationships, resulting in troubled relationships one after another. Her next entry seemed to indicate these inner emotional struggles were transferring onto the men in her life clearly noted by her next journal entry.

Why can't I forget about you? Why does this part of me just hold right on? Won't let me forget, just constantly reminds me of your face, your eyes and how much I miss your touch, how much I miss your love. Am I just in denial or do I really feel this way? I know I'm not happy. I have fun, but I don't feel happy. I cry out, but only my constant fears answer back. I feel lonesome, unloved, even though someone wants to take your place, it's not the same. I want to feel the same, but I don't; I can't. Or maybe, I just won't let myself feel. All I feel is the anguish of not being with you and each day comes with a new hardship, new battle. But I am tired of fighting. It's an endless tyranny with unsuspecting victims. I want no part; want to just leave with you.

This shit is really getting to me. Every time realization slaps my cheek; gives me a wakeup call, a reality check. Everything clears for an instant, then clouds right back up. I miss those days; the ones so far away, completely out of reach. Addiction to a drug I can't get my hands on, but when I close my eyes I see it! I long for it! And I miss it so dearly! I just want to break down, but addiction is wrong, and I'll be okay. The days just soar by and I just watch instead of fly. It's driving me crazy, completely insane. There's this unsettled mess just laying inside me, beside itself with boredom. It longs to be free and fulfill my dreams instead of just dreaming them. I know what I want but am lost and can't seem to get there. Each day a new frustration, but I will still flourish and greet each new frustration with the smile of determination. I will succeed!

November 5, 2005

As a child, I called it homesickness because I was away from home visiting friends and I couldn't stand being away from home all night. But now I no longer get sick from being away from home. But I do have the same feeling. I think of you and it's the same exact way I felt at eight when I couldn't stay over at my friend's because I missed home-my mom. But I haven't felt that since I was eight. I don't understand why life works this way at all. I just want to be happy. But I just can't seem to get there, not without you. I cuddle up to the man I'm with now and tears well up. It's so hard. And I miss you so much. It feels as if my heart can't break anymore. Maybe in time everything will be right. I hope so.

November 13, 2005

I need someone who appreciates me; someone who won't take me for granted; who will love, honor, cherish and make me realize how special life really can be. I can't look at your picture without lovesick pains aching not just throughout my chest, but my whole body! My body just aches for you. It longs to be held and caressed. Kissed and loved like it once was. It misses the contentment and all-around love we shared. I just can't get over everything that I miss. It's insane to think of how often I think of you and keep my distance still.

As inevitable as our breakup was seen by me, I didn't believe such heartsickness was also a consequence of my actions; my attempts to bring the best to my life instead of continuing the way I was going. I really didn't think I'd lose so much of the one thing I've always truly desired, happiness.

I see how much of it I really did have with you. And realize the good things much more than the bad. God, I miss that face Those lips, tongue, eyes and hands. I miss your chest and legs as our bodies entwined as we so peacefully slept. I miss you so incredibly much; your voice and laugh. That wonderful charming smile and way that you would be.

I miss those awesome times we shared together. I thought there were many more in store, but I'm afraid it's really over. I haven't stopped loving you or thinking about it all day, every day. You're constantly on my mind. What do I do? I'm lost without you.

I've never felt this cold before, so alone. Not a day passes when I don't think of you and just break down. I need you here to help put me back together. Everything is so different. I don't even know myself anymore. I just crave your touch and pacify my needs with things that remind me of you. I bought Men's deodorant because it reminds me of your smell. I miss your scent; that intoxicatingly sweet, I know I was right where I belong, smell. And I have no idea where I belong. Each day so different yet all the same. Each time I miss you as soon as I feel that lovesick pain. I close my eyes and my mind takes me to you. to our precious moments that are now my deeply cherished memories.

God, I loved you. Loved you more than even I realized. I cry for you more and more each day. But you never answer my cries. And the tears I shed seem endless as my loneliness. Why does it have to be this way?

They say if you want something bad enough it will happen. But you're still away from me and I need you more than ever. I need to feel your arms wrapped tight around me and your lips everywhere. I need that love - that passionate crazy endless love that you showered me in day after day.

It's like you're a drug and you've got me addicted. I could never get enough of you. You really did love me so and I see everything clearer now. I want to be with you, to be in love. I want kisses and affection and that deep intense wonderful love that you gave me.

I feel as if my heart is slowly turning to ice and you are the only warm thing keeping me from being completely frozen. Just knew that I love you dearly and even though I'm with him I still long for you because his love isn't half as passionate or half as meaningful. You would truly die for me if needed and I would do the same for you.

November 16, 2005

I thought I had moved on to bigger and better things. But each day I find myself wishing for the way things were. For the love, I used to have. The love I have now is just no real love at all. It's fighting and anger and all the things I've been running away from my whole life. I feel like a whore. A useless, pathetic female only suitable for one use. Even my sanctuary fails to console as it once would.

I cry each and every day, just like I always have. But if I could choose whether to have stayed or left my love again, I would never have left. I'd rather be homeless and loved than "taken care of" and *abused.*

This gray, cold dreary day matches my present outlook extremely well and well, I'm right back at square one. I need to make some new plans. There's two sides to the monster-one side is the cover up because this is no average monster. He conceals its true self in order to gain trust from its victims. Once gained it lashes out to first consume its victim emotionally, therefore increasing its power for the final kill.

I don't know how much longer I can keep playing these insane games. I'm so tired of them. I don't want to play anymore; just want what's real. I just need to feel loved again, to feel affection. I say I don't need men, not even he, but there is one even though he's no longer in my life. He's still playing one of the most important roles to me. My memories keep him so close and pacify my desires. I remember. But of course, I do. How could I forget?

The love we shared was real, know this because it keeps me going still. He never gave me close to half of the physical things I now receive, but...he gave me one hundred times of what I'm getting now of all the things, all the money in the world could still never buy such precious and valuable gifts. And that's what love's about. Not money or "things." It's about LOVE. And he was never afraid to love me. You're terrified!

I'll be going now because I need, and you won't give ~~*. I miss that heart pumping heavy breathing, pure excitement, joy and happiness. I miss the closeness, the trust. Once we realize what we had it was like no one could take it away because it was purely ours. No one of course, but ourselves. And that's what I did-gave up the only man I'd ever loved to be miserable and treated like a prisoner. Such irony. Gave up my man while he's imprisoned only to create and live in my own twisted little prison. We put ourselves here. It is so sad. But I will BREAK FREE!

Sarah~

~

REFLECTIONS

Sarah's words ruthlessly thrust all those painful memories back at me, forcing me to remember all those moments, all those things I had tried so hard to push back, set aside with the intent to refocus—redirect—channel my thoughts into positive ones, positive energy, rather than that negative and poisonous place where I once lived, where we all lived, caught in a place where I never ever want to be again.

My heart squeezed as I felt the pain of those angry, dark days, freshly, starkly. I was transported back to see our ravaged family through the lens of a thirteen-year-old girl, Sarah's eyes. Why wasn't I stronger and wiser? A lot of what happened between father and daughter, I did not see. Then again, I knew-didn't I? How could I not? Who was this weak noodle of a woman who allowed her husband to bully and tyrannize his family?

I am a time traveler transported back to the past; thrust into an environment I struggled to escape. The quarreling, fighting, and mean-spirited, spitefulness. I would stand between father and child trying to break up arguments. Sarah and I were confronting him, and he hated it!

However, I could not always be there to intervene, to mediate, to soothe egos, smooth ruffled feathers, to protect. We were all so angry then. I felt defeated and hopeless; stuck in a place where there seemed to be no way out. Money was always a huge problem, or better described, lack of money. His control seemed absolute, emotionally and financially.

Caught in the perfect storm of manipulation and control; a faith which taught that a wife must be submissive and obedient to her husband to promote peace within the household. If she questioned her husband's dictates and methods, she could face chastisement if the husband complained to the elders that his wife was not submissive or in my husband's words, was difficult and uncooperative.

Men in the congregation, appointed as elders, were chosen for their spiritual maturity and insight. Elders accepted the responsibility of shepherding the congregation. Their insight was based on scripture, using the bible to counsel, encourage and offer solace, as they interpreted scripture according to their faith. During one such house call, two elders were visiting us on what is known as a shepherding call. Just before they left, I implored them for validation of my revelations. Their expressions bemused, one of the elders asked, "What do you mean?"

"I simply want reassurance that you believe me; that my confidences and concerns are valid."

He shook his head as he told me, "I am not a professionally trained counselor."

There was no validation. There were no words offered to comfort me or recognize my emotional pain and tearful admissions or the fear and stress I and my children were experiencing and had been experiencing for years. His words deflated me, causing me to feel disrespected and without worth. I had opened my heart, but as they left our home I felt deeply wounded. How can one receive validation if the spiritual counselor does not recognize or even understand the term? As they turned away and left, I felt alone and unsupported.

A huge chasm opened inside of me, a void I simply did not have the ability to define. Years of expressing high esteem and respect for the elders in our congregation began to crumble that day. The entire fabric of my life began to unravel—threads dangling, disconnected.

I recognized their sincerity. I also recognized their limitations realizing they were, after all, just men, not demigods. The insight I garnered that day was this. These men, pillars of the congregation, positioned to offer help, guidance, and counsel to their flock, of which I had been part of for decades was ineffective, futile and condescending, at least for me. Did they consider me resistant to God's teachings? It was not God's teachings that were the issue; it was how these teachings were interpreted and applied.

Manipulation of my thoughts had caused me to drown in self-doubt and indecision. Years of exposure to biting sarcasm and belittling and controlling behavior had resulted in a complete eroding of my self-esteem. I gradually became a woman who felt too stupid to accomplish anything. Though I continue to struggle with these feelings, I now can define them, identify them and override them.

I eventually recognized, with counseling, I needed to get a backbone. I was helped to realize I was a woman of substance who did possess intelligence. I stopped retreating from conflict. I began to find my voice and I learned how to use it. I gradually began to take back what I had allowed him to usurp; some control of my own life, and something much more important—self-esteem. Albeit, too little, too late.

I had not realized how deeply I had buried my memories. It is so much easier to cope with the present by trying to forget the past. Why dwell on unpleasant and painful memories? I simply could not. The shame—the pain was just too great. Tucking them away allowed me to maintain a sense of equilibrium. Filing them into forgotten pockets of my mind helped me to find the strength to survive the onslaughts of life that never seemed to end. So many deaths, so many tears. My parents, my younger sister from breast cancer, her only son at age thirty from a brain aneurysm, and now... Sarah. All of them leaving this earth too soon.

Facing my own health issues, emotionally and physically, have been challenging as well. No, I am not seeking sympathy or pity!

Forget that! Life is packed full of choices and decisions that can never be changed. With each choice, we exact a result we must own.

I cannot dwell on the *if only(s)*, so I try to concentrate on the present, on loving and accepting my kids for who they are, despite my own flaws. My focus has redirected. Blessed with grandchildren and offering them our support and love has become a priority. So many lives, so many needs, so many smiles and hugs. There is already enough negativity in the world. My intent is to provide a little less.

The damage to our family is irreversible. Our remaining adult children carry their memories with them and will do so for the remainder of their lives. Rather than dwelling in the past, I can only recognize my life choices, accept my mistakes, try to learn from them, striving to become the person I was meant to be. Life is precious and fleeting—too precious to focus on regrets.

If I have learned anything at all, it is this. Accept that we are the person we are now because of our life experiences. Strive for growth in this process we call life. Reach out to engage with others within our little circles of humanity. We all are individuals with unique qualities and strengths. All of us experience heartache and tragedy. Instead of burning our bridges, we need to build them strong and resilient to withstand the depredations of life. Humanity's strength and tenacity is amazing, especially when we recognize we are not alone! We are all joined by a common tether—our humanity—our love.

My perspective is narrow presented through the lens as a grieving mother. It is limited to one who has lost a daughter to addiction. A mother should never have to experience finding her daughter as I did. It is unthinkable. However, one thing is different. I know more than I knew before Sarah died. Why must tragedy occur to produce insight?

The road leading to addiction and the reasons one succumbs to substance use disorder is long and winding. Addiction is complex and those who struggle with it usually face other mental health challenges too. They struggle with loss, loneliness, pain, and emptiness. They long for fulfillment. They feel misunderstood, misjudged, stigmatized, unloved. These voids must be filled. The human spirit demands it.

As Sarah pursued her education, she became more aware of the social injustices that surrounded her, forcing limitations upon so many. I think she empathized more deeply for others because she was fighting hard to overcome her own. Sarah's discernment and mindset were clearly evidenced through her journal entries. She accumulated many journals which she wrote in over the years, but I cannot possibly include all her entries. To be frank, many I chose not to include. Many of her entries were so personal, I will never share them. Nonetheless, I must share her final entry, which she wrote a few short weeks before her death. This entry defines how dark her world had become, her anguish. It was her final missive directed toward her boyfriend who had died from an accidental drug overdose, three months prior to her own.

November 6, 2016

Someone from your family deleted and blocked me off your Facebook. It really sucks to not be able to share like everyone else and communicate – makes me look like I don't care about you – or think or want to have anything to do with remembering and celebrating your life. Kills me that I got cut off like this. But I grew up with disfellowshipping and although the pain isn't easier this kind of treatment isn't new. It's exactly what I'm used to.

Sarah~

Authorities say her death was also due to an accidental overdose. I beg to differ. She was driven, goaded, and bullied. Her boyfriend's family threw their own guilt upon her until she simply could not live with her emotional pain. His family, crazed with grief, anger and bitterness, blamed her for their son's death, despite the fact that he had a long-standing history of substance abuse, long before he ever met Sarah.

They sent her threatening messages—crass, cruel and wounding. Messages left on her phone and on her Facebook page. Messages expressing clearly their wish that she had been the one who had died, not him. The messages were filled with hate. They expressed their wish that she would die! Sarah forwarded some of these messages to the mom of her best friend, a friend who also had died from an accidental overdose. We were attending a grief meeting together when she told me she had the messages on her phone. Shocked, I asked if she would share them with me. As I read the words, my mind clouded over with incredulity. Anger washed over me in a wave of heat as I read, *"Die, you fucking bitch!" Why don't you just die! We hate you!"*

The final blow to Sarah's heart? They deleted her expressions of love and loss and then blocked her from her boyfriend's Facebook page. Well, they got their wish. I do not know if it brought them satisfaction. I do not really care. It does not matter because I refuse to go there. I project no ill wishes toward them, but can I forgive them? I am unable to answer; perhaps in time. Perhaps never. I don't know. I am healing. I hope they continue to heal as well.

They lost their child, just as we lost ours. To lose one's child in death, no matter how or why is incredibly painful and life changing. I am terribly sorry for their loss. Are they experiencing their own private hell, their own regrets, perhaps their own wishes for do-overs? Who knows? Life is harsh. There are no do-overs. Time travel does not exist allowing one to go back and re-write their future. We build our own futures with every life decision. The hate these people spewed toward my daughter is...unforgivable.

Highly educated individuals with doctorates publish papers full of information, facts, and figures, explaining reasons for addiction. It is often good information extensively researched and properly cited. I do not have a Ph.D. or a doctorate. I am simply one who loves to teach, write, and more importantly, a mom who loves her family. I majored in motherhood. I minored in English.

Sadly, I lost something most dear to my heart, my daughter's voice. I only hear her voice as echoes in my mind, and as I read her journals. Her journals are full of her—her voice, worries, goals, sadness, hopes, desires, disappointments, happiness and love. Her writing identified her feelings, but they do not clearly define her as a person because her life was so much more. How to define, articulate her essence, her multi-dimensional personality?

As I wrote this story it took on a life of its own. Prose, narrative, and dialogue interweaved, allowing not only the reader but also the author to peer into the looking glass, to see beyond oneself to what lurks in the background of the human soul. How special each of us really is. We all deserve to be loved and to be recognized for the good we do, for the difference we make by just being.

There are huge gaps when Sarah did not write. Her happier moments? Were they moments spent studying and attending classes? Moments when she felt loved and in love? I will never know why or where she was in her life journey during those gaps, at least not completely. And that is okay, because she was living more fully during those times. She was happier then.

It seems that when her world became dark and hopeless, she used writing as a means to purge all these feelings. Her own personal therapy, just as I have done this past year. Nevertheless, I know this. She did make a difference while she walked on this earth in a myriad of wonderful ways.

~

Sarah, you are missed and loved. I love you forever and always!

~

HOME

May 20, 2017

I need grounding. Sarah's words are too much for me. Time to take a break. The sojourn into the past demands balance. I return to the present. To my reality. I'm glad now I decided to read Sarah's words when I wasn't alone; when I was doing domestic, normal, everyday stuff that grandma's do.

Today, I am at Sherry's home. She and her husband, Derek are away for four days. In Florida. Heat. Humidity. Family. Another funeral to attend—Derek's brother has died, leaving a gaping hole in his sister-in-law's heart. Of these things, there is certainty. Humanity. Birth. Life. Death. Regeneration. I firmly believe death is not the end.

We are given a gift—the wonderful, precious gift of life while here on this earth. What we make of this gift is up to us, but as we walk through our life, then pass on to the next step, who knows what God has in store for us? No fear.

I close the laptop craving normalcy. Something comforting. I look in the pantry to find a box of brownie mix. Yes, something sweet. Chocolate. The kids will like it, but to be honest, I want to fill the house with the homey, delicious scent of baking. I need to feel a mixer in my hands and taste the sweetness on my tongue to erase some of the painful bitterness I just transcribed.

I want to see my grandkids finally come out of their rooms and talk to me as we snack together. I too need to feel loved, appreciated. I also need to let them know I am expressing my love toward them. I want to make a memory for them, like my Nana made memories for me.

I fill the pan with thick chocolate batter and swirl it just so, then placed it in the oven to bake. The final touch is to frost them with my specialty—chocolate buttercream frosting. Sugar rush. The best cure I know for the inner child in me and for the sobs that I refuse to shed today.

An hour or so later, the brownies, cooled and frosted sat on the counter top. Allison and her brother, Sean emerge from their rooms and sniff the air. They smile.

"Do I smell brownies? Are they ready yet?"

"Yup! I responded."

We cut them and eat them with cold milk. Yum. I walk out on the back deck to stand at the railing facing the pond. A pair of mallard ducks swim leisurely by leaving small ripples behind them. The male duck's bright green head is distinctive and handsome. A bird, high in a nearby tree talks to me then breaks out in song.

"Is that you Sarah?"

Signs of life, love and energy surround me. The sky is so blue—deep and ongoing. I spy what looks like an eagle or perhaps a hawk soaring high above. It circles the area then flies on. Sounds of a chain-saw, not too far from here. Someone is cutting down a tree. Crabapple, cherry, plum and lilac trees are blossoming, sweet and fragrant. Bright yellow dandelions going to seed, releasing their white fluff to drift on currents of spring breezes. They float around me, white and filmy. They resemble jellyfish that float and bob in the sea, only these float and bob in currents of air spreading their seed. Spring. New life erupting. Even as I try to say goodbye to one lost, there is always newness and vibrancy. Energy. Allison comes inside to get her sneakers. Lacing them up, she turns away to leave, her words trailing behind her. "I'm going to ride my scooter."

She is thirteen, but still such a little girl. I was glad to see her out of her room, away from her TV and her iPad. I remind her, "Don't forget your helmet."

"I don't have a helmet."

She quickly walks out the door leaving no room for argument. Definitive. I like that.

Laughter. Sean is in his room listening to a political satire. He is sixteen, growing up quickly. When Heather was sixteen she already had her first baby boy, Sean's cousin; both sixteen now. Reality. Everyone faces his or her own realities. Realities made from choosing and sometimes just because.

Sean walks by me. "I'm bored," he utters. He wanders toward the door to go outside, but then he quickly comes back into the kitchen.

I turn toward him to repeat his statement, only as a question, "So, you're bored?"

He retracts his utterance. "No, I'm not bored. I'm having a brownie."

He cut himself another piece and took a bite. "These are really good."

I smile. I have not lost my touch. Their cocker spaniel, Buddy, leaps up resting his paws on the side of the kitchen counter, a weak attempt to steal the brownies. Clapping my hands, I say, "No!" He quickly turns, looking guiltily toward me then slinks away into the living room, his head hanging low. I give him a doggy treat instead. "Here you go."

He gobbled it down quickly and looks askance, hopeful for another one. "Nope, just one."

His brother, Jax, a King Charles Cavalier Spaniel snoozing under the table perks his ears up. "Yes, Jax, you get one too."

Late afternoon. Time to make supper. The kids are hungry. Grounding. Family.

I whisper, "I miss you Sarah."

Goosebumps dimple and raise on my arms. I hear her laughter in my mind. She is never far from me. She lingers, her memory. Her essence. Sarah's energy. She is free to roam, explore, and be where she wants to be now. I choose to believe that she is in that place of eternal love, the place she searched for while here, on this earth.

Sadly, many do not realize something; before one can love another in the purest form, one must love themselves. It has taken me a long time to recognize that this elusive thing called love takes many forms. When young, we fall in lust, I think. Then, if it works out, and if we are lucky, lust evolves. Changes. Becomes richer, warmer. It matures into this elusive thing called love.

Once, a long time ago, when Sarah was emerging from the chrysalis of childhood she asked me, "What is love?"

I do not remember what I told her at the time. How could I forget such an important moment? If I were asked that question now though, I know what I would say. Forgiveness. Patience. Acceptance. Realizing our humanness. Our imperfections. Cradling a sleeping infant, caring for a sick child at two a.m., teaching a teenager to drive as you counsel, "Hey, easy on the brakes. My back isn't young anymore." Then patiently explaining how to come to a smooth stop. Working long, hard hours to feed your family. Getting a call in the wee hours of the morning from your child, whether a teenager or an adult pleading, "Mom, I need your help. Can you come and get me?" Then, getting up, going out, and just saying, "I'm glad you called. I'm glad you're okay."

Sarah was unable to traverse the muddy waters of teenager into healthy adulthood. Somehow, caught in the byways where darkness loomed, she just could not get away. It enveloped her. Washed over her. Overcame her.

When I first began to write this story, I shared it with a grief counselor. She came to my home to talk. About to leave, her gaze swept up the stairs to see the blue curtain I had hung in the window. She observed the Chinese lantern and wind chime hanging below. The window was open, and the summer breezes were causing the chime to sing.

I watched as her gaze lingered, then she turned towards me to say, "Please don't hold onto the guilt. I believe that your daughter's inner struggles began when she was little, perhaps the day when she held her arms up to her dad while you held her in your arms. It seems the father/child bond never took hold between them. I am so sorry."

She paused before leaving and said, "I too am forever changed by your story."

Although I was not aware of it then, those words placed a seed in my heart. Only now have I become aware of this seed and its effect—it introduced something significant; the first step in the process of healing.

Now, although she is gone, Sarah walks with me, and I with her. We are closer now than we were when she was here. Does that sound strange? Odd? Her journals have given me new understanding, insight. I speak to her in my mind, words of endearment pass between us as I tell her every day, "I love you Sarah!"

I hear her voice as she whispers back, "I love you too, Mom. You always did make the best brownies."

Echoes. Memories of her horseback riding and the huge smile she had after one of her lessons or trail rides. God, she loved that horse, Sebastian. I am not sure who rescued whom though. Sebastian or Sarah? Sarah or Sebastian? They rescued each other I think. Yes!

It seems like yesterday when Sarah was just thirteen and given the responsibility of caring for Sebastian. Horses helped to ground her. It was a good time for her, a happier time. However, as with all things in our lives, things change. Sebastian, a rescue horse, was neglected before Sarah met and fell in love with him, and he was an older horse. Despite Sarah's loving care, his health never fully recovered. He eventually died. The equestrian center's owner later sold the business and moved out of state.

College Essay

It seems that small discoveries are revealed when I most need them. I recently found an essay Sarah wrote for one of her college classes. Not surprisingly, her chosen topic to write about was her equestrian center moments. Full circle. Sarah, now a young adult reminiscing, shares some of her happiest moments. Her essay is not dated, but I do not need the date to recognize when she wrote this essay.

My First Love

Summer is a long-awaited delight for those that live in a climate such as the state of Maine. The air takes on an intoxicating odor, especially at the barn, which I called home throughout the majority of my teenage years. My mornings started much earlier than they do now, and I miss starting my day hearing the soft knickers of hungry horses eagerly awaiting their morning grain. The stall cleaning was my meditation time. I spent several hours each day reflecting back on events that had happened and planned what I was going to do with myself.

I chuckle at myself when I remember how I was one of those little girls that always wanted a pony. It seems so unrealistic today because we have cars to drive around and horses are a hobby to the well-off persons in this world. Growing up in a good-sized family that was not very well off, to say the least, proved a challenge since my hobby required substantial investment and expensive maintenance. My mother's reply to my begging for a horse was to find me a job at a new horse boarding and training facility. I did not realize it then, but my mother did me one of the biggest favors in my life.

My job at the barn was very rewarding for me to say the least. I simply made sure all the animals were fed and watered and that the barn was thoroughly cleaned each day. Once I turned fifteen, I was getting paid, in addition to a lesson each week. The owner of the barn also wanted me to start working with her young horses. It was here that I thrived on the successful progression of my riding skills. I believe it was due to this very kind and positive woman that always seemed to know how to encourage me. The owner of the barn had taken somewhat of a special interest in me and surprised me one gorgeous summer day by announcing "my horse" was in the trailer headed up the driveway.

The truck came slowly up the driveway pulling a bright red horse trailer containing the first horse that I was told I could call my own. I was thrilled and could not wait to see what my new mount was like. The man who was delivering my horse slowly backed him off the trailer and gasps escaped from everyone watching. The driver passed the horse's lead rope to me and said, "Meet Sebastian."

As I took it, I looked into Sebastian's sad, but kind eyes. He returned my gaze and nudged my arm with his nose. One could easily count each of his ribs and his hipbones were sticking out. His eyes were sunken in from starvation. He was an older gelding with various health problems, but I did not see all that. I brushed his long forelock out of his eyes and I knew that he needed me as much as I needed him, and he became my first love. "Everything is going to be a lot different from now on," I whispered to the gelding as I led him to his new home.

The next few months were spent with careful feeding regimens aimed to get Sebastian at a healthy weight. Due to him being so underweight, he could not bear the weight of a rider and all my work with him was done with me on the ground. I set up an exercise plan that gradually got him back into shape and eventually I was able to start riding him. Each free moment I had, I spent either playing follow the leader out in the pasture, for he loved to follow me around because he knew I always had a treat for him in my pocket or grooming him until every knot was out of his tail and his coat was flawless. I fell in love with his kind nature and was amazed that even though he had been abused so severely he was not hesitant to share his love toward me.

It was amazing to see how far Sebastian had come in the past few months and to be a part of his exceptional progress.

My favorite rides on Sebastian were on the trails through the fields and woods surrounding the farm. We would gallop through the fields and although we were separate entities, it was on these special moments that I felt as if we were one. I felt completely exhilarated with the wind rushing through my hair and all I could hear was the hooves pounding the grass Beneath us.

Thankfulness

How do I express how I felt as I read Sarah's essay? I cannot, at least not fully. My heart swelled with thankfulness and gratitude for Sarah's expressions of happiness and accomplishment. Things I hoped she would experience when I first spoke with the equestrian center's owner when I left Sarah there that first day.

I watched Sarah as she blossomed and grew in self-confidence. Her smiles and willingness to rise with the sun to get to the barn were evidence enough of her commitment, pride and joy. Sarah's essay helped me to realize something else. I did good. I was a good mom. She loved me.

My Observations & Realizations

Sarah's journals caused me to observe many things. She craved that unconditional love all children need from their dad, but tragically she felt she never received it. She widened her search. Young, still naïve, she was unable to tell the difference between lust and love, how others will take advantage of you, use and abuse you. These life experiences, I believe, resulted in her inability to commit, even when she had found someone worthy of her.

When she did finally meet someone who just may have been the right choice, she kept him at arm's length. When she realized that she was ready and traveled to tell him so, he had moved on. He was now with someone else, even though he admitted he still had feelings for her. Her initial response? Anger, sarcasm. She learned well.

He came to her memorial service, his warm brown eyes glistening with tears. He came with his girlfriend, a tall, statuesque, blonde-haired woman who looked uncomfortable and wary. She resembled Sarah. He introduced himself. "Hi, I'm Sarah's friend, *Michael.* I am so sorry. A friend told me what happened. I cannot believe she is gone. She called me just before..."

He could not finish his sentence. His voice thickened with emotion. I looked at him dazedly and asked him, "Before? Before what?"

His gaze focused just beyond me as his own memories resurfaced.

"Just before I heard she had died. I cannot believe this. I do not understand. We had just talked; we were making plans."

He seemed to have forgotten for a moment the woman beside him. I glanced at her face, and then looked away. Her small smile had faded. She glanced away too.

I had no idea at the time who this man was. Nevertheless, I recognized sincerity. I recognized grief. His sadness touched me as he hugged me. His name—I do not even remember. Later, when the brain fog cleared, and rationality returned I remembered things. I remembered Sarah speaking with fondness of a man who lived a couple of hours north near Bangor as she described him.

"He's an RN. He's really sweet and I think he likes me."

I never knew what happened between the two of them. I just know what did not happen—they never seemed to make that connection. She traveled up there several times to see him, but for some reason I was unaware of at the time, a committed relationship did not develop.

One day, Sherry and I were talking as she revealed, "I've been communicating with *Michael.* He really misses Sarah, mom. He feels she lingers nearby; he feels her energy too. Did you know she had planned on introducing him to you and dad?"

My eyes widened in surprise. "No, I never knew that! Why didn't she?"

"I think she was fearful of how dad would have reacted if he knew she was dating a black man."

Uncertain of how to respond to this statement, all I could say was, "Oh, Sherry. I wish she had brought him to the house. He is such a nice man. I would have welcomed him! Who cares how your father may have reacted."

Sherry's eyes held mine, "Sarah cared, mom. She was fearful dad might have been insulting or hurtful. She did not want to put *Michael* in such a position."

My thoughts lingered on this conversation. Would Roger have reacted in such a way? Jehovah's Witnesses are taught to treat everyone with respect, regardless of race, culture or skin color because we are all descended from the same parents. This faith expounds the need to accept their *brothers and sisters* despite their heritage. Sarah's own paternal history had affected her deeply leaving ingrained fears of how her father may or may not have reacted, particularly involving her choice in men. Sadness washed over me.

Full Circle

Today, near the end of May, I'm here, in my daughter and son-in-law's home. Here… in Maine. Yes… I came back.

"I have unfinished business," I told my sister before I left.

Brinna looked at me with an understanding only sisters possess as she said, "Yes, you do."

Packing finished. Brinna, I and Donnie climb into her car to head for the airport. After six weeks away from home, Donnie decided it was time to pay a visit to California.

I needed a vacation, mom. California seemed like a great place to visit. I've never seen the Pacific Ocean or the Redwoods either."

"Really?"

"Well, yes!"

"No other reason to come out here then?"

"Grinning widely, he admits the rest of his truth.

"Alright, I admit I came to get you. I figured if I came to California, you'd be more inclined to come back home, especially if I was accompanying you."

My son, so wise.

So, here I am, back in Maine. My place of birth. Home. My children. My grandchildren. My husband. My heart. Emotional conflict continues. Healing continues. And. Walking the pathway leading towards forgiveness continues. Ongoing.

A lump, hard and painful, rises in my throat as I think about all that has happened, but I force it down as my grandson, Sean comes back out of his room and wanders around the kitchen opening the refrigerator and then the cupboards.

"Hey, Grammy, when are we eating?

I close the laptop again, gently, as I look up at him. I smile at this boy morphing into a man who is always hungry and tell him, "Soon."

One's Inner Dialogue

Each of us struggle with our own inner dialogues, often challenged by anxiety, depression, anger. Perhaps we should dig deeply into our inner hearts. Scientists have studied the mind intensely. The brain consists of millions of neurons, which are wired together and fire together. When one dwells on certain thoughts and feelings, this memory or thought process grows stronger and is more easily triggered; creating a pattern of thinking that is difficult to overcome.

So, what happens when a young girl feels rejected by her father or mother? Perhaps she perceives them to be disinterested, disconnected emotionally. Perhaps she feels her feelings are ignored. She senses her parent's irritation whenever she is in his/her presence. Perhaps a parent ignores their child's plea for help. Patterns of behavior are difficult to change. The emotions evolving from these scenarios, whether real or imagined, can cause deep emotional pain and thoughts, similar to my daughter, Sarah's, creating an inner dialogue of negative self-talk.

"I'm not loved by my dad (or mom.) If he doesn't love me, then I'm not worth loving or helping. He's mean. I hate him."

If one fails to recognize these feelings as compulsive thinking and does not work on stopping them, these feelings become more and more ingrained over time. I believe this is what occurred with Sarah.

Unfortunately, this science was not available to me twenty years ago. If it had been, perhaps I would have been better equipped to recognize what was occurring. Knowledge brings power. This knowledge could have empowered me to try to stop my own compulsive thinking. Could I then have helped Sarah to identify with hers as well? Both of us were stuck in a loop of endless inner dialogue that kept these negative emotions alive, causing them to grow stronger and more imbedded.

Thus, armed with this newfound knowledge I recently shared it with Heather because she and her family are nesting here, in our home for a little while. Is six months, a year considered a little while? I believe, in the scheme of things, it is. Because life is a river that flows. Sometimes dams get in the way and must be scaled. Sometimes floods occur washing over you. Sometimes we just make choices that need to be accepted, learned from. Sometimes we are so overcome with grief, we need help to heal. I am a parent who has learned a hard lesson. Life is uncertain. I am determined to be there, to be supportive, and when the time comes, allow my child to move on as they become strong again.

Meanwhile, Heather and I are reconnecting, grieving together, speaking of Sarah every day. Talking about her and our grief, our loss, how adrift we feel. I'm watching, observing, connecting. I am being a mother. Heather needs me, and I need her. We hug, a lot! We cry, a lot! We are... .family.

Once, Sarah told me something that I dismissed, or more accurately, took rather lightly. I will not dismiss her thoughts, nor those of my remaining children again.

"Mom, you are the matriarch of this family. You have a lot of power, you just don't recognize it yet."

It is possible to teach ourselves to become mindful; to catch ourselves as our thoughts begin to formulate and recognize we have a choice. Do we continue the loop or break it? We do have free will to decide. We can become wiser, more mindful of directing our thoughts to become healthier and more positive.

THE GIFT OF SARAH'S LETTERS

May 2017

Sitting in a café, facing the window, I'm aware of cars as they cruise by the window. The skies are gray. It is raining. I sip my mocha latte, savoring it. Chocolaty, warm and soothing. I am alive. There were moments when I thought about joining my daughter, wherever she may be. My guilt was at first so heavy! Sadness lingers—it will be a part of me until my time here to walk this earth has ended. Until then, I am surviving the sadness and grief. I am not home, in my room, shut in; shutting out the world. I have not taken to my bed.

More importantly, I am not silent! The time for silence is gone. The time of averting one's eyes to the reality of addiction is past. The time of stigmatizing those who struggle with this terrible disease must stop. The time to advocate for those who cannot advocate for themselves is now. I want to shout. I want to scream. Sarah lives through me and I will be Sarah's voice.

Meanwhile, the days come and go, merging from past to present, and then simply slip away until one day, I entered Sarah's room. My eyes focus on her dresser sitting flush against the wall. A compulsion to look in the drawers urged me forward. I knew Sarah's sister,

Sherry, had already gone through them, packing away Sarah's belongings several months ago, a few weeks after Sarah had died. I watched as Sherry opened the drawers one by one, emptying the contents onto the bed. Clothing, papers, a notebook. A medley of things. Lotion, a square, black textured cosmetic case. Sherry set this aside and asked, "Mom, do you mind if I keep this?"

"No, I don't mind. Keep it." I turned aside to brush away a stray tear. Sherry went through Sarah's things meticulously, deciding what was important to keep. I could never have done this alone. Sherry's presence was comforting. As we did this our ears hummed. The air was heavy with energy, sadness.

Today, Sarah's room again hummed with energy. It is difficult for me to describe, but not sadness this time. This energy felt different. How do I describe it? Intense? A sense of urgency? It seemed to be pulling me in, urging me toward the dresser. I opened the top drawer on the left discovering a pile of papers. I pulled them out and started going through them. Somehow, they had gone unnoticed. Among the papers were three letters. Each letter stapled closed on the ends. The letters were written on white-lined notebook paper. Each letter individually addressed. One letter addressed to me, another letter to her dad, and a letter addressed to both of us. Our names written artistically, the letters filled in with purple and blue. A lot of thought and time, love were dedicated to these letters. Letters not received until now. Five months out from Sarah's death.

I sat down on the edge of the bed, Sarah's bed, the bed I sleep in now since I returned from California, because it gives me comfort and eases my pain. I moved my clothes and my desk in here where I sit and write. I hung a collage of her images on the wall beside the desk. I put my clothes in her dresser, but I did not notice the papers!

I found a painting rolled up and tucked away in her closet. I unwrapped it and discovered something beautiful, captivating, and special. A huge moon descending from the sea, casting its luminescence upon the water. The backdrop? A black and endless night sky filled with countless shimmering stars. The artist's name? Chad. It was dated 2015. Who was Chad? Perhaps I will never know. Why had

I not found these letters? These precious letters, these gifts of love suddenly revealed, overwhelmed me with emotion. *Oh, Sarah. Thank you! Thank you!* I opened the letter addressed to me first.

Rising Moon by Chad

June 23rd, 2015

3:56 am

Dear Mom,

Thank you for making me breakfast and checking up on me today. Thank you for voicing your concerns and suggesting solutions to care for my health. Thank you for offering to go to the store just to get me a muffin! :-) That was so incredibly sweet! (and totally unexpected!)

Eternally grateful for you coming to pick me and my car up at that ungodly hour. I'm sorry I used another AAA tow up for the year. Hate being a burden!

Thank you for helping me with gas and insurance and feeding me and basically keeping me clean and alive.

I do need more hugs though.

Love, your baby, Sarah

I began sobbing in earnest, gasps of sobs. The kind of sobs I had not allowed myself to express yet. Grief and love intermingled, washing over me in a huge wave. Drowning, engulfing. I am allowing myself to feel this intense pain and longing for my daughter, fully, completely. Her words bring me solace and realization of her love for me. Healing had begun. Could I achieve self-forgiveness?

June 25, 2015

3:42 a.m.

Mom and Dad

Thank you for successfully rescuing me in the wee hours of the morning. I will never forget and would/will (but hopefully not have to) return the favor. Thank you for letting me stay through these trying times while I get my life together.

Greatly appreciate your support despite that I do not express enough at all—even though I feel grateful to have a home to come home to every night and parents that love me. Am lucky and blessed to have you both.

All my love, your baby, Sarah

P.S. Sorry for being such a shit-head sometimes.

My tears blurred her precious words. I furiously wiped them away. Letters from Sarah! She left us a wonderful gift. Her voice filtered through, expressing her love and gratitude. Why had the letters gone unseen?

The third letter was for her dad. I descended the stairs to the living room where he eternally sits, on the loveseat, watching TV. I handed him the letter unopened, still stapled closed on each end. He looked at me with a question in his eyes.

"What is this?"

"Letters written by Sarah."

I showed him the other two letters. "I found them in her bureau beneath a pile of other papers."

He opened his letter. As he read, tears, cleansing and long unshed filled his eyes, overflowed to course down his cheeks. His body shuddered with his own sobbing. He had cried little since Sarah's death, at least not in my presence. His sobs filled the room. I sat beside him resting my hand on his arm. I have been so angry. So. Intensely. Angry. At him. At the world. At me. He deserves compassion too. I opened my arms and tried to offer some comfort. For now. We sobbed together.

June 23rd, 2015

3:54 a.m.

Dear Dad,

Thank you for coming out in the wee hours to rescue me. Thank you for being there for me financially while I'm trying so hard to get my head game on point! (In case that last sentence was confusing, I meant basically mental health.)

Thank you for helping me with gas and health insurance and doctors' appointments and gas to pick the kids up. It really cheers me up when I get to see the kids and I couldn't do it without you.

[The kids are Sarah's nieces and nephews—Heather's children. Sarah loved them deeply. They were her world.]

Thank you for putting a roof, food, and all the physical needs you meet for me every day. Thanks for being there for me through these confusing, overwhelming and trying times. Your support means the world.

Love you! Love, Always, your youngest daughter, Sarah

We had received a gift—completely unexpected! It was as if Sarah had reached out to us from beyond the veil to reassure us, to remind us that she loved us, loved her dad. We will never know why she did not give those letters to us two years ago, but instead put them away in her drawer, where they lay hidden, until I found them five months after her death.

Sarah's Letters

IN THE DARK

However, the letters invoked a two-year-old memory. A night that provided signs that Sarah was in trouble. The phone rang at two a.m. waking me from a sound sleep. It was Sarah. "Mom, I'm really sorry to call you, but I ran the car into a ditch trying to avoid hitting a deer. Can you please give me the information, so I can call Triple A for a tow? One more thing. A police officer is here, and he will not allow me to drive the car home. Will you and dad please come?"

She gave me directions. She was on a back road far out in the country. Her directions were sketchy, and we made a wrong turn. Realizing that we were going in the wrong direction, we called her again. She was having difficulty relaying clear directions, so I asked to speak to the police officer. He explained where they were more clearly. By the time we arrived, the tow truck had her car out of the ditch but had refused to leave. He wanted physical proof of insurance. I got out of our vehicle and walked over to speak to him, handing him the AAA card. Taciturn, surly, he nodded his head, fired up his tow truck and left.

Meanwhile, the police officer talked to Roger. He explained that Sarah's registration had expired, but he was giving her grace to take care of it. He also kindly explained that she was shaken up and he thought it best if she did not drive.

The drive home was rough. Sarah's face was pale. She was tired, irritable. Patches of early morning mist rose from the fields and woods shrouding us in ghostly white ground fog. I was not used to driving in the wee hours of the morning or driving her car, so I drove slowly. Sarah became argumentative and defensive. I was tense, tired, concerned and felt my own walls of defensiveness erecting as I caught myself snapping back at her.

It was dawn before we finally arrived home. I parked her car in the driveway, turned off the ignition, opened the door and walked toward the house. Early morning light met my upturned face, as I listened briefly to the sounds of birds chirping, goats bleating, and a cock crowing. I watched as Sarah's long legs took her quickly up the steps and into the house. By the time I entered, she was quickly climbing the stairs to her room.

Late afternoon, near suppertime Sarah came downstairs. I was in the kitchen. She walked by me, her face ashen, her lips white. She was shaking with chills. I looked at her with concern.

"Are you alright? Are you sick? Can I get you something?"

She shook her head no. "I'll be okay. I have to go out for a bit, but I won't be gone long."

I noticed her talking on her cell phone as she headed for the door. I was surprised that she was leaving when she seemed to be sick.

"You're sick. I don't think you should be leaving feeling like this," I told her.

"I'll be fine. I'll be back in a little while."

She was true to her word. She returned an hour or so later. When she came home, she appeared to be feeling better. Her color was good. She did not have chills anymore. A miraculously quick recovery.

I relayed this all to Roger later and asked him, "What do you think?"

He shook his head, "I'm not sure."

We were her parents, but we did not accurately interpret or acknowledge the truth. Uneducated regarding addiction, we were unable to clearly identify that Sarah was struggling with opioid addiction and what we had observed were symptoms of withdrawal. We were in the dark.

A SIGN

JUNE 25 2017

Determined to push through boundaries preventing me from recovering from grief, including where I found Sarah I claimed Sarah's space as my own a few days after I returned home from California. Her bed envelopes and comforts me. Her essence surrounds me.

Tonight, though I am restless. Glancing at the clock, I notice the time. Three a.m. Swinging my legs over the bed, I slip my feet into my slippers. Standing, I stretch, muscles tight, and open the bedroom door. The small hallway is flooded with soft moonlight. I head to the bathroom. Returning, I shut my door, climb back into bed, plump my pillow, lie down willing my tense muscles to relax, then close my eyes.

The room is dark, the blinds closed tightly. The window fan hums softly, surrounding me with white noise. I roll to my side; moments later, I am on my back again. I feel a soft flutter, a touch, light as a feather upon my cheek. Opening my eyes, I see movement above me. Shadows really. What appears to be a dark outline of a winged creature flutters near the ceiling above me. Startled, a bit fearful, I turn on the light. Nothing is in the room, nothing at all. Leaving the touch lamp on low, I opened my door to hear all the normal night sounds. It is four a.m. Yawning, closing my eyes, I awaken a few hours later to bright sunshine.

The following night, lying in bed, again willing myself to fall asleep, I sense a presence. How do I find the words to describe something incredible? The night when Sarah came to explain to me what I had actually seen and what it represented.

The following weekend I struggled to describe to my eldest daughter, Sherry, the experience. It was twilight and she had made a fire in the pit. We sat in her Adirondack chairs placed around the fire pit. Not looking at me directly, but gazing into the fire, her words caused self-doubt to rise quickly in my heart.

"You know, there is a condition that some people experience when they are deeply grieving. It's called grief-induced psychosis."

"So, you think your mom is crazy?"

"Of course not, mom."

Nothing more was said, and the conversation turned to other things. The warm summer evening. The ducks quacking and emerging from the pond looking for bread crumbs. The blue heron suddenly appearing to stand on a fallen tree slightly submerged in the water. The peepers as they welcomed another summer night with their frenzied high frequency sounds. A dog barking in the distance. Smoke from the fire, lifted by the summer breeze billowed briefly around us.

Her simple phrase, "grief induced psychosis" lingered in my mind, filling me with unease. Nevertheless, I knew what I had felt. What I seen. How deeply comforted I was that night, as I lay in Sarah's bed, and how I more easily drifted off to sleep afterward.

I believe I was given a sign, a gift of love, comfort. I was unable to fall asleep the following night after seeing the winged shadow, my sadness omnipresent. As I laid in bed, tossing and turning, a sensation of love, deep and endless enveloped me. My restless movements stilled. I felt as if I were in a warm cocoon. Love filled my entire being. There was soft, joyous laughter. Then words, not heard audibly, but rather sensed inwardly.

"I have my wings, mom. I have my wings. I'm your angel and will always be nearby. Be happy. I love you, mom!"

Speak of a conflict of emotions! Wherever I go, Sarah is with me...always! *I love you too, daughter of mine. My angel.* Sarah had given me a sign. Strength to go on, move through, continue my own path, set goals, strive to meet them. To make a difference. To love. To forgive others and myself. To toss away, fling it far, far away—misplaced guilt. Sarah would want that. If this was a type of grief induced psychosis; well, better this than feeling helpless, hopeless, and wanting to die too.

A PROMISE

Long ago, Sarah asked me for a promise. This forgotten memory suddenly resurfaced. Sarah and I were walking together as she paused near a bench to ask, "Do you want to sit for a moment?"

We sat side by side, her long legs outstretched, our shoulders touching. Birdsong surrounded us. Mid-summer. A soft breeze blew a strand of hair into her eyes. She brushed it away. I was silent. Watching her. Waiting. Sensing something was on her mind.

She turned towards me searching my eyes before she spoke. "Mom, I know how you feel about pot, and smoking it goes against your principles, but this is important to me."

A pause in the conversation ensued as I shook my head in affirmation, but said nothing, waiting for her to continue.

Her voice was soft, earnest, purposeful. "Promise me something, Mom?"

"What is it Sarah?"

"Promise me that if I die before you that you'll stand over my grave and smoke a joint in my memory. Just a puff." You don't have to smoke the whole thing."

A child is not supposed to die before a parent. It was not something I could even consider. I refused to accept the possibility. However, I felt the need to respect her request just the same. As I gazed into her eyes on that long-ago summer day, I saw something that scared me. Something I rejected then and did my best to forget. She was only twenty years-old and she was talking about her death, not jokingly but in all seriousness.

Laughingly, I responded. "Well, that's asking something, but that's not going to happen! I'll be gone long before you, hon."

"Mom, life is uncertain. You never know. So just humor me, okay?"

"Sarah, if you should die before me, I will try to do this. But, I don't even know how to get marijuana."

"Well, I do," she said.

We both laughed, as I responded. "Yes, I know you do."

Sarah's pink marble urn rests at her sister, Sherry's home, lovingly displayed on a lighted shelf in their family room. During this intensely emotional time, Sherry made a request, or a statement really. "Mom, I want to keep her with me always."

We simply could not bury her remains, at least not yet. Perhaps next spring after the snow melts? Perhaps as her birthday approaches in April? Perhaps when daffodils and tulips emerge from their winter sleep and lilac trees blossom with their fragrant purple blooms? Perhaps in May or June when the air turns warm and green grass covers the ground with its soft carpet? Perhaps. So, there is no final resting place chosen. As time passes, and our pain lessens, that will no doubt change. Deep within me something stirs. A yearning for closure. A need to do something meaningful, special. Sarah loved the ocean. Splashing through the waves at sunset was her favorite thing to do. I have never smoked anything, including pot, in my entire life. Can I fulfill this request from Sarah?

Sunday, September 3, 2017

Waking early, I hear her voice in the deepest recesses of my mind. Sarah's voice has been silent for a while now. My reality? I am busy, continuously busy. Keeping busy prevents me from dwelling on the grief that is always just beneath the surface, ready to bubble up and over. When it comes, I allow myself to feel it fully, to release the tears. So many things remind me of her, and that is okay. Somehow, I know today is the day. She is close, and she wants me to finish this. Closure. A new thought fills my mind. A message of maturity, wisdom. I know it comes from her. How? Impossible to explain. I just know. "Be true to yourself, mom."

These words filled my mind like a mantra. Falling asleep the night before and then awakening in the morning, the words repeated, an echo, a voice recorder on replay. Was I receiving a message? I have learned to open myself rather than remain closed.

Sarah understood my reticence to smoke marijuana. Do I really need to do so to honor her memory? She does not yet have a gravesite. What would mean the most to Sarah? Family. Our entire family finally doing something together. Setting aside the differences and the drama that seems to ooze into every corner of our lives. Heather and her family are here in our home today. Sherry is but a phone call away, as is Donnie. Decision made. I step outside onto the side deck to make the calls as I stress my need to do this today.

Donnie answers my call to reveal he is working. He works continually now. It's Sunday, yet he seems to fill almost every waking moment with work. I seldom see him. My concern for him is omnipresent. Has he taken the time to process and come to terms with his sister's death?

I explain why I am calling. He pauses a moment before responding. He confides in me a recent incident. His voice chokes. I listen as he pours out his own grief. Several days ago, he escorted a client to the emergency room. While there a young woman was brought it. She had overdosed. He described how he was instantly transported back to that day. The day Sarah died. "Mom, I don't know what came over me. I started shaking. I've never felt like that before. All I could see was Sarah's face."

His grief hit him just like that. Grief can be sneaky. It sits in wait, patiently, silently. When you least expect it, it reminds you of its presence. It must be recognized, affirmed. To heal, one must ride the wave. It picks you up, then releases you, sometimes softly, but this day it slammed him—hard. Recognizing the need to allow himself to grieve, he asked for a week's leave of absence.

Sherry and her husband are at first reticent, but recognize my need, our family's need to come together with a common goal. Closure. Standing outside on the deck, my focus is drawn towards the field on the far side of the road. The tall grass sways with the afternoon breeze, the tree line just beyond. Coniferous trees scattered among birch, maple, alder and elm.

Heather, Sarah and I sometimes walked out there in the woods when they were little girls. A memory resurfaces, bubbling up, frothy, beautiful, of a stream with rocks scattered in the middle meandering through those woods. As we hiked, we crossed it one day jumping from rock to rock. Sarah slipped and got her sneakers wet. Worriedly she looked at me as if I would be mad at her. I laughed instead and joked that we finally had a good excuse to get her new sneakers. Suddenly all three of us were laughing. Two little girls, blond hair, fresh and new, their lives just taking shape.

Refocusing on the conversation with Sherry, the memory recedes as I continue our conversation. The goats are bleating behind us where our nearest neighbor has a small farm. "Sarah would be ecstatic to see us all together as a family. She wanted this to happen so badly."

"Yes, I know, Mom." Sherry's voice was low, thick, full of emotion as she asked,

"What time do you want to meet?"

We set a time. Satisfied with the arrangements, I opened the door to the kitchen and went back inside to fill everyone else in on my plan. Heather and her family were staying with us for now as they worked toward rebuilding their own lives. Home hunting. Healing. Reconnection. Reconstructing the bridges that had begun to crumble in our fractured family. We have spent long hours talking, rehashing, reminiscing, and holding each other as we cried expressing our grief —not alone now, but together.

Fort Popham

Heather's children frolicked and laughed as they ran through the sand near Fort Popham. They dipped their toes into the frigid Atlantic. Waves rolled relentlessly toward the shore. They crouched closely toward the sand looking for shells, flotsam, memory makers. My grandchildren. Sarah's nieces and nephews. Sarah loved them all for their uniqueness. Their childish glee lifts my spirits and fills me with love. So much love!

The sun is setting over the water casting its shimmering glow. The sky above beautifully streaked with purple, mauve and pink. The cloudscape is magnificent. I gaze around me, taking in our surroundings. The pier loomed nearby and the waterscape beyond it held lobster boats, dipping and swaying to the swells. The sun making its slow descent would soon be gone from view.

We have chosen a picnic table close to the water, its surface weathered and grey. Sherry draped a corner of it with a purple-fringed tablecloth, gently placing Sarah's pink granite urn upon it. She and her husband, Derek had released some of her ashes from the urn into two small cut glass jars with sealed stoppers. I pour the fine white ash, all that is physically left of Sarah, into several small white plastic cups.

A sweet herbal smell surrounds us as Sherry begins to burn Angelic Incense and sage to cleanse the air and to lighten our thoughts. She believes the incense allows one to ask the spirits to help us gather angelic forces and to bring angelic power to us. The sage will clear the air of negative energy and allow space for the spirits to enter our aura. Sarah would be pleased. Heather was impressed. "I see you are returning to your roots," she said.

Sherry laughed. I watched them share a sisterly moment, glances between siblings, glances revealing a bond they were attempting to rebuild too. Forever practical, I wondered if the incense will also chase away some of the voracious mosquitoes swarming around us. Dusk was quickly descending. It was time. Sunset.

My plan was for us all to walk the beach, as Sarah had done countless times during her short life. I had hoped to retrace her steps toward the waves, releasing Sarah's ashes upon the water, but access to the beach for someone with limited mobility such as Roger's is challenging here. The pier is only a few yards away. It will do. Heading toward the pier, we make our way to the end, Roger leaning heavily on his cane. We all turn to face the setting sun, each of us carrying a cup containing some of Sarah's ashes. Looking toward my family I make a request. "Would anyone like to say a few words?"

I've surprised them. This event was last minute, a whim of their mother's. They are unprepared. They stare back at me, momentarily frozen, unable to speak, overcome with emotion. Roger stares at me, soundless, mute, his eyes wide, blank. He is doing this because I insisted. How does he really feel about this moment? I do not know. He did not say, and I did not ask.

Raising the cup, I find my own voice. "Sarah, we love you and miss you so much. You will forever be in our hearts."

Sherry's voice follows mine as she swallows her own grief. "I love you so much, Sarah. We miss you so much! You know, we are here today because of mom. She knew how much this would mean to you —having all of us together. Mom listened to you Sarah."

I counted to three and together we released Sarah's remains into the sea, her favorite place to be. A sea breeze carried a tiny bit of Sarah's remains back toward me, caressing my face. Heather and Tierra, mother and daughter, hold each other, their tears falling, mingling, dropping into the sea below, our DNA, joining with Sarah's ashes, to forever be a part of our precious Sarah.

A large bird appears overhead, its wings spread wide, as it circles above us, dipping its wing in salute. The sun's last rays reflect briefly off its form. It seems to glow. It turns, flying above the sea towards the setting sun. I watch it as it becomes a mere speck, disappearing into nothingness. Lifting our cups, we fling Sarah one last tribute as my heart tightens and swells with emotion. Grief. Sadness. Love. "Well, Sarah. We did it! Together at last!"

Is that the sound of laughter way off in the distance? Gulls can sound like laughing children I have been told. Signs. If we look closely, they are all around us. If we close ourselves to possibilities, then we miss them. Choices. Do we open our hearts or close them? Hearts can be shattered. Hearts can mend too. Scar tissue, tough and resilient forms around the wound. When tugged, it will be painful, often for a long time. Then, something miraculous happens. Healing. Life. Love. Laughter.

Out of the corner of my eye, I glimpse a form. My mind's eye sees her. Sunset. Her arms are outstretched holding her red butterfly shawl. It is fluttering around her caught by the wind. Her back is turned facing the waves. Her hair lifts and then settles softly around her shoulders. She walks into the sea.

The sun makes its final descent disappearing beneath the horizon. Darkness began to settle. Mosquitoes voraciously whined all around us. Ignoring them, we closed ranks. Group hug. Tears. Laughter. Swiping away our tears, we packed things up, and climbed into our cars. My window was open. The sea breeze, fresh and cool dried my tears, lifting my spirits. Turning my face toward the ocean I watched the waves as they crashed against the rocks. A lone seagull swooped and dipped on the currents of air. I fling words of love out to the universe.

"I love you Sarah, always and forever."

THE NATURE OF ADDICTION

As a mom who has lost a daughter to accidental overdose, I faced a dilemma. Should I choose to grieve in silence and shame due to the stigmatization of addiction and when asked how she died, respond vaguely or, should I be truthful about the way she died? Judgements. Yes, people judge, especially those who have not experienced what my family has. Someone addicted, especially to heroin, faces monumental challenges by society and their families are judged right along with them. Who ultimately is responsible for the untimely deaths linked to opiate addiction? Some would say it is the addict. Others might hold parents, accountable. However, as time passes, and knowledge accumulates, truth emerges, evolves and grows.

There were 378 deaths in Maine in 2016 connected to opioid and fentanyl overdoses. My daughter, Sarah was number 376. Approximately one death a week across the state of Maine in 2016. Nationwide there were more than 4200 deaths related to opiate addiction in 2017. That number in Maine increased in 2017 to 418 and 247 deaths were directly linked to fentanyl. This disease, identified as Substance Use Disorder, is decimating much of Sarah's generation. It does not discriminate. It crosses all socioeconomic borders. It is a wave encroaching upon our society, affecting almost everyone in some manner or form. While being treated by a physical therapist a conversation ensued about addiction. His stated, "It affects physicians, nurses, and other medical personnel. Almost anyone can be susceptible." Opiate addiction reaches into our homes, our families, stealing away loved ones and peace of mind, leaving a trail of grief and broken hearts.

A score of my daughter's friends and associates had fatally overdosed before her. A person with a healthy mindset can recognize danger when it confronts them and take appropriate action. Addiction changed Sarah into a person we no longer knew or understood. Changed her mindset, her ability to recognize danger and to react accordingly.

Twelve years ago, many things happened. Sarah became ill, underwent surgery, and she was prescribed opiates for her pain. I had joint replacement and also was prescribed opiates for pain control. I developed an allergy to opiates. Lucky for me. Sarah was not so lucky.

Sarah's addictive personality was unknown, unidentified. Should physicians have asked about our family history before prescribing addictive opiates? My family has a long history of alcohol addiction; four generations long. Physicians had not asked, before prescribing me pain medication, if there was a history of addiction in my family. Not once!

Did my daughter have a choice at age eighteen to accept a prescription for pain? What about the physician who prescribed an addictive medication to a teenager? What is his accountability? Physicians did not educate their patients then of the addictive properties of opiates before prescribing it. Pharmaceutical companies knew how addictive opiates were and how quickly some people could become addicted, but they kept this knowledge to themselves, not informing the medical community.

For many, it can take only two to seven days to become addicted to an opioid. During that time, the brain changes. It develops an insatiable craving that demands to be satisfied. Once the brain is sensitized and the addictive process begins, the stigma projected towards those with substance use addiction significantly reduces the likelihood of the person seeking treatment. The stigma of addiction is destructive, deadly, life destroying.

Some feel that ignorance is bliss. No! How can one protect themselves or others from potential harm if they are ignorant and unknowledgeable? How can one react appropriately if they do understand or recognize the signs? I was blissfully unaware during all those years of Sarah's struggles until it was too late. Sarah's death opened my eyes to the existence of a world circling mine, sometimes touching, but I somehow remained clueless, unknowing. No longer. Forced to recognize its existence, to make a difference I needed to educate myself. Knowledge is power. Knowledge, when used well, save lives.

Many questions linger. In order to invoke lasting change, they must be addressed. How do we approach this complicated and all-encompassing opiate issue? Why are the drugs pouring into our country with such ease? Why does the government fail to be more proactive in stopping the influx of drugs, including dirty heroin (heroin muddied with other substances including fentanyl?)

The constitution of the United States of America is founded on this principle. *A government by the people, for the people, of the people.* If people join ranks, insisting that the government directs its power towards eradicating the influx of opiates and other deadly drugs into the country, will this affect positive change?

The purpose of sharing our family's story was not intended to become a political statement. Nevertheless, society is faced with a crisis. Scores of people are dying, and the numbers are increasing. This is an epidemic so encompassing the implications are terrifying. What is more terrifying is there is so little attempt to stem it.

Yes, there are mumblings, posturing by political elements, but what is the end result to date? I do not profess or to offer answers. But I do present questions. An epidemic should cause humanity to join forces, to combine their individual skills, knowledge and fiscal resources to identify and invoke a plan of action. Yes, this issue is complicated and challenging but does that indicate it cannot be overcome?

We must look outside the box, outside our country, and observe how other countries are approaching the issue of opiate abuse. If citizens as a whole insist that the government allocates adequate funds to meet the increasing need of timely and adequate treatment to those with substance use disorder what may happen? If schools, universities, healthcare clinics, etc. were also allocated funds to initiate programs to educate communities about addiction what may happen?

Even more importantly, expanding medical coverage is imperative. Currently in Maine, there is little hope for those struggling with addiction for the uninsured because they cannot afford and/or are refused treatment. Hopefully, this will soon change as Maine's newly elected governor takes office. Regardless, treatment facilities are limited in Maine, especially due to the rural nature of this state. Therefore, insurance coverage is simply not enough. Maine must also increase the amount of appropriate treatment facilities. Expanding treatment options through expanded medical coverage and increasing options for adequate treatment will save lives. My daughter may be alive today if these options had been firmly established.

Reducing access to opiates is only the beginning. What if government programs were formed with the sole purpose to educate, inform, and offer support and compassion with the intent of lessening the stigma attached to addiction? We must arm ourselves with knowledge! Can we end the stigma of addiction and stop the dying? Yes, I believe this is possible, or at the least, we can lessen death by overdose.

Currently, Hamilton County in the state of Ohio is providing free narcan, which if given soon enough can reverse an overdose. This is showing promising results in lessening death by overdose. However, those who receive the narcan must also be trained in its proper use. A person who has overdosed must receive narcan within minutes or it will be too late.

The opioid crisis is far from over. There is still much to do. Lessening the stigma attached, providing adequate insurance, access to appropriate and timely treatment and educating our youth are all actions we, as citizens must advocate. We must use our voices. Stop the silence. Stop turning our faces away. Much of a generation is dying. It is shameful, heart-rending. So much fear, so many tears.

~

ADDICTION - CHOICE OR DISEASE

Offering Hope

It is a common misconception by many that individuals struggling with addiction made a choice. They chose to swallow that pill, sample that first beer or other alcoholic beverage, eat sweets, or any other substance that can be addicting. In a world where addiction is rampant, technological and medical advancement has made discoveries that fifty years ago were not common knowledge or perhaps not even thought of. Thus, we must become informed about this silent disease, rather than making judgements often based on ignorance or even bias.

Scientists and researchers have been delving deeply into the cause of addiction and how the human body works, including the brain. Yes, some would say we are living in a brave new world. However, I prefer to recognize our world as changing, evolving and becoming more informed of how our bodies and minds are affected by environment, heredity, social norms, culture and family structure because all of these things intertwine making us who we are, and we are definitely complicated entities.

Researchers have discovered something that brings hope to the addicted. They believe strongly through scientific evidence that drug addiction is a disease. What facts give credence to this statement? As a mother who lost her daughter to addiction, I needed to know why. I needed affirmation, perhaps even validation of the true nature of addiction to help me maneuver through the grief and begin the difficult process of healing.

Curiously, some people try drugs or alcohol and never get addicted. Others, however, have a biological or situational predisposition to addiction. Unfortunately, our family history without doubt played a part in my daughter succumbing to addiction. Several individuals in my family tree are confirmed alcoholics, including a brother, uncles, and a maternal grandfather. Possibly, there were others, but at least four generations of my family have struggled with addictions. Situationally, my daughter struggled with mental health issues as well. To add to her risk factors, our family life was dysfunctional.

Once a person begins using, the addiction takes on a life of its own and is much harder to control. As I became more informed, I came to realize my daughter exhibited signs of addiction and dependence on many substances, including alcohol and marijuana, as well as opiates. Her feelings of low self-worth and social anxiety increased the prospect of developing addictions. I know that now, albeit far too late to help my daughter, simply due to my own ignorance and life distractions. In sharing what I now know, it is my hope my readers will be inspired.

I believe it is best to present things simply and briefly. I am not a researcher or a scientist. I'm a mom who has experienced a traumatic event, that of finding my daughter in her room, no longer breathing, facedown, her fingertips blue. In my grief, I began my own research.

The simple truth is this. Addiction is a disease because it causes changes to the brain. Not only does it create a physical dependency in which the individual cannot stop taking the substance without experiencing withdrawals, but it also affects the individual's ability to make reasonable decisions. How do drugs change the brain?

Every drug, including alcohol, disrupts the reward system in the brain. Unfortunately, long-term usage can cause changes in the reward circuit that influence the brain's ability to function. Specifically, the areas of the brain tied to making decisions, learning, remembering, and controlling behavior. A paper, published by R. D. Baler and Nora D. Volkow (both from the National Institute on Drug Abuse) stated, "There seem to be intimate relationships between the circuits disrupted by abused drugs and those that underlie self-control [...] the time has come to recognize that the process of addiction erodes the same neural scaffolds that enable self-control and appropriate decision making."

Media states we are in the midst of an opioid crisis. In order to save lives, it is imperative we become informed. We must recognize what is going on all around as we become more engaged, mindful and observant, whether it is of our children, a friend, or someone manifesting symptoms of overdose in a public restroom or in sitting in a vehicle in a parking lot. Doing so will save lives. For many years I was ignorant and in denial. We no longer have that luxury if we seriously want to prevent someone from dying, leaving a void in families and in society. There is no doubt that the death of a human being who entered this world with potential causes immeasurable loss.

Remnants of Heroin Use That You Might Find

Heroin is usually smoked, snorted or injected. Depending on the method of administration, you could find remnants of the drugs or the paraphernalia of drug use left behind. (We found syringes, a burned metal tube smelling of smoke. Rubber tubing. A blackened spoon.) Observe if you are missing excessive amounts of spoons from your flatware. Heroin itself may be a powdery or crumbly substance, ranging all the way from off-white to dark brown. Black tar heroin is nearly black and is sticky instead of powdery.

You might find syringes, small glass, or metal pipes. A person dissolving the drug and injecting it might also leave dirty spoons and lighters around. A person injecting also needs some device to cause the veins to enlarge, so there may be belts or rubber tubing found in the area where he or she is using the heroin.

Heroin is a fast-acting opiate. When injected, a surge of euphoria occurs within seconds. Those using the drug other ways may not feel this surge as sharply.

The user will get a dry mouth and his or her skin will flush. The user's pupils will be constricted. The person will feel heavy and dopey and may fade in and out of wakefulness. Heroin users may nod off suddenly. Breathing slows, which is how an overdose can kill. When awake, the person's thinking will be unclear. They will tend to lose some of their memory. Their decision-making and self-control are likely to deteriorate. This is the condition I discovered Sarah to be experiencing the first time I found her as I heard her labored, slowed breathing two weeks before her fatal overdose.

Other signs of heroin use are itching, nausea and vomiting. Another sign of heroin use could be constipation. Sarah manifested with all of these symptoms as well. I thought she had a flu. The regular user of this drug may look for laxatives. They may experience skin infections, or other kinds of infections, and a lowered immunity to illness.

Signs of Heroin Use and Drug Paraphernalia

Burnt spoons, Tiny baggies, Tan or whitish powdery residue, Dark, sticky residue, Small glass pipes, Syringes, Rubber tubing, spoons containing residue or blackened marks.

Possible Appearance: Tiny pupils, Sleepy eyes, Tendency to nod off, Slow breathing, Flushed skin, Runny nose.

Possible Actions: Vomiting, Scratching, Slurred speech, Complaints of constipation, Complaints of nausea, Neglect of grooming, Failure to eat, Covering arms with long sleeves.

My daughter seldom covered her arms with long sleeves, but we often observed slurred speech. Sometimes I would hear her vomiting, and often she did not want to eat. There were times when she exhibited unusual sleepiness. I was uninformed, naïve, and never in a thousand years could consider that my daughter struggled with opiate/heroin addiction. The signs were there. I just did not recognize them. Perhaps subconsciously I did, but I simply could not accept the truth, until one day in December, our world came crashing down around us.

CONCLUSION

Writing this story has reaffirmed several things for me. Life is a gift; something to be cherished because it is fragile and can end in a heartbeat. Life is about making memories, cherishing loved ones, maintaining friendships. I want to build bridges rather than walls, to open doors rather than close them. Allowing myself to feel, process and move through the grief has invoked the beginning of healing. Recalling Sarah's words, I am reminded of how intelligent she was. "Drugs are like false promises; vacations from reality. Unhealthy, self-defeating behavior. Encouraged to destroy the impoverished so they can keep all their wealth and wield the power that accompanies it."

Intelligence has nothing to do with addiction. I understand that now. I also realize I am not alone, and it is okay to reach out and say, "I need you; I need help." Let's work toward allowing everyone that opportunity, including those struggling with substance use disorder, ending the stigma. As I processed my grief coming to terms with Sarah's death, I have reached another conclusion. I realize that a perfect family is also an illusion.

Slowly, I am relinquishing much of my guilt, and am working towards forgiveness. The process of healing is slow though. Can I forgive completely? I do not know. All I can say is I am trying. I am human. Sarah is dead. However, I am determined her death will cause an impetus to invoke change. Hence, I have shared my story with the hope that by relinquishing our secrets, others can begin their own journey of healing, forgiving, loving. It is terribly important to express our love toward those we care about. Love is the greatest gift of all. It defines our humanity.

"Love bears all things, believes all things, hopes all things, endures all things. Love never ends." I Corinthians 12:7-9

SOURCES

1. DEA Drug Info/Drug Data Sheets/Heroin, retrieved April 2017, https://www.dea.gov/druginfo/drug_data_sheets/Heroin.pdf.

2. DEA/Pubs/Abuse/Drug Data, retrieved April 2017, http://www.justice.gov/dea/pubs/abuse drug_data_sheets/Heroin.pdf.

3.Drug Abuse/signs of Heroin Abuse, retrieved April, 2017, http://www.narconon.org/drug-abuse/signs-of-heroin-abuse.jpg.

4. Drug Addiction: The Neurobiology of Disrupted Self-control, Baler, R. D. et al., Trends in Molecular Medicine, Volume 12, Issue 12, 559 – 566, retrieved April 2017.

5. Finding True Refuge (2015). The Opportunity of "The Magic Quarter Second." Tara Brach.

6. Methoide, retrieved April 2017, http://methoide.fcm.arizona.edu/infocenter/index.cfm?stid=214.

7. NIDA (2003). Preventing Drug Use among Children and Adolescents (InBrief). retrieved April 7, 2017, https://www.drugabuse.gov/publications/preventing-drug-use-among-children- adolescents-in-brief.

ABOUT THE AUTHOR

I proudly profess to be a lifelong native of Maine who obtained a Bachelor of Applied Science Degree from the University of Maine at Augusta where I studied English, Creative Writing, Education, and Library Science.

Reading was my first love and I spent uncountable hours visiting my childhood library where my imagination ran wild. Exploring the stacks of reading material at libraries stirred within me the desire to write my own stories.

Writing helps me process my world, articulate my feelings, and express my imagination. My specific genres of writing include memoir, creative nonfiction, fiction and poetry.

I love walking along the various shorelines, listening to the gulls and the sound of surf rushing toward the shore then retreating. Sunsets and sunrises call to me because of their ever-differing hues and cloud formations. Sarah loved, as do I, walking a beautiful trail known as Hobbit Land by our local community. Children imagine mythical creatures dwell there, and love exploring as they run through the woods where tall white pines grow dropping their soft needles below in hopes of finding their hidey-holes and perhaps a chance encounter.

The walking trail leads through the woods down towards a stone bridge spanning a rocky stream presenting with a small waterfall just beyond. Beautiful and peaceful, the sound of flowing water and the pungent scent of fresh pine infuses me with renewed energy and hope, refreshing my soul.

May you always cherish the magical and memorable moments as you pursue what brings you joy and peace.

Ann Bennett-Cookson

Author

Messenger address:

https://m.me/AbennettCookson.author

Website address:

https://mainelywritingsweetthoughts.godaddysites.com/

amazon.com/author/annbennettcookson

twitter.com/Ann@23607629

facebook.com/MainelyWritingSweetThoughts@abencook

A FEW WORDS FROM THE AUTHOR

Dear readers:

Thank you for purchasing and reading Secrets: A Story of Addiction, Grief & Healing. Please take a moment to leave a brief review on Amazon. Reviews are extremely important for independent authors like me as well as potential readers. Your thoughts are important in many ways. They allow for growth, improvement and encouragement for authors and they encourage others who are searching for literature offering content important to them. Sharing this story with the world was a difficult decision, one not made in haste. It was written in the midst of deep grief.

When a child dies, no matter what the cause, grief can be paralyzing, overwhelming. However, with an overdose death, the stigma attached to addiction often induces emotions that a grieving parent should not have to experience. Guilt, remorse, self-recrimination, and shame. Currently, our society generally induces a measure of shame, stigmatizing those struggling with addiction, having a rippling effect upon families.

Slowly however, I came to realize it is possible to survive heartrending loss such as this. During this process I did what writers do. I threw myself into writing, and began journaling in an effort to process and better understand the "why's and how's" and a way to stop agonizing on the "what if's."

Over the next several months, a story unfolded as I blended Sarah's words with my own using her journals which she had tucked away, unaware at the time this was the beginning of my journey toward a measure of healing. I was determined to be completely transparent in sharing our story. Secrets: A Story of Addiction, Grief & Healing was completed less than a year after Sarah's death.

Please visit my website at:
https://mainelywriting.com

May you walk in light and peace.
~Ann Bennett-Cookson~

www.ingramcontent.com/pod-product-compliance
Lightning Source LLC
LaVergne TN
LVHW051503080426
835509LV00017B/1893
* 9 7 8 1 7 3 2 2 5 8 9 1 4 *